D1250192

# LETTING GO AND FINDING YOURSELF

VERENA KAST

# Letting Go and Finding Yourself

## Separating from Your Children

Translated by Vanessa Agnew

CONTINUUM • NEW YORK

1994
The Continuum Publishing Company
370 Lexington Avenue, New York, NY 10017

German edition Copyright ©1991 by Verlag Herder Freiburg im Breisgau
English translation Copyright ©1994 by The Continuum Publishing Company

Printed in the United States of America

Library of Congress Cataloging-in-Publication Data

Kast, Verena, 1943–
     [Loslassen und sich selber finden.  English]
     Letting go and finding yourself: separating from your children /
Verena Kast; translated by Vanessa Agnew.
        p.     cm.
     ISBN 0-8264-0655-6 (acid-free)
     1. Empty nesters—Psychology.    2. Parent and adult child.
3. Separation (Psychology).    4. Identity (Psychology).    I. Title.
HQ1063.6.K3813   1994
155.6'46—dc20                                            94-5185
                                                              CIP

# CONTENTS ......................

# Foreword

♦

SEPARATING FROM ONE'S CHILDREN is easier to live through if one pays attention to the process and consciously says goodbye.

Although separation is inherently painful, much of the pain can nonetheless be avoided by focusing on the process. This book arises out of such thoughts and experiences, and I hope that it will be helpful in drawing attention to this special grieving process, that it makes it both easier to understand and withstand.

A book such as this arises out of the shared experience of all those involved. But we ought not forget that in some respect we are all involved in this process.

I would like to thank the women who allowed me to tell their stories about the difficult journey of separation. Their stories are typical of many. I would like to thank them for their willingness to entrust their experiences to me for the purposes of publication.

I am very thankful for my daughter Renata, who with much love and perseverance, produced the final draft of my manuscript.

*Verena Kast*

# Getting Involved and Letting Go

◆

"ARE SEPARATION PROBLEMS WOMEN'S PROBLEMS?" asks Annemarie Stüssi in a newspaper article entitled, "Separation Begins in Kindergarten."[1] "Certainly to some extent," she answers. "Because men are engaged in their work, as a rule they have less difficulty dealing with such situations, and are consequently less often confronted with feelings of emptiness."

It is well known that women whose exclusive role is that of the mother generally have great difficulty dealing with the departure of their children, since ultimately it has to do with the loss of their main purpose in life. It has also been proven that these women respond to separation from their children with depression, while women who have not exclusively devoted themselves to their children are less prone to depression.[2] Separation is a problem.

However, is it really only problematic because these women have no profession, no other central purpose in life? And what can be said about those women who do indeed have fulfilling jobs, but who nevertheless experience the separation from their children as very painful? And what about the men, who also suffer tremendously when their children leave home, and who do all they can to get them to stay?

Separation problems are not just women's problems: they are human problems. However, since women usually get totally involved in the relationship with their children, separation from these children and from this involvement can become a central conflict leading to crises and ensuing reorientation.

As human beings, we have to get involved with other people, and yet we also have to let them go, which is the very thing we find difficult. We must learn to let go in such a way that we do not just feel bereft; let go in such a way that we will have the courage to become involved again, even though we know that getting involved will imply having to let go, with all its contingent pain, and will also imply the urgent need to reorient oneself. An emptiness remains whenever a person with whom we have been closely involved goes out of our life. We can try to fill up this emptiness as quickly as possible; we can replenish it. Alternatively, we can pause and ask ourselves whether emptiness is the only thing we feel. Aside from the emptiness, is there perhaps a thankfulness to be felt, perhaps joy that a phase of life has past? Are there, for instance, feelings of guilt that are surfacing? We can also ask to what extent space—freedom—now exists. What fantasies does the emptiness conjure up in us?

Each process of separation throws us back on ourselves: we are alone, we are left behind, perhaps we are even lonely. An inexorable question emerges: Who are we, and who might we be, if we can no longer define ourselves in terms of our customary, familiar relationships? This reorientation demands self-awareness, yet the process also affords a new self-determination.

# Separation Processes

◆

WHEN SPEAKING OF SEPARATION PROCESSES in the context of children, typically we think of adolescents[3] who leave home and move in with roommates or into their own apartments. Generally they turn to people who have become more important to them than their parents. This separation process in adolescence has to do with the most incisive separation process between parents and children. It is a process of great importance, since in leaving home the children learn how to separate and the parents, in turn, have to learn how to let go.

But separation processes begin much earlier and accompany the entire course of the relationship between parents and children. Indeed, separation processes accompany all relationships; getting involved, letting go, and getting involved again—sometimes getting involved again at a new level—are rhythms which are a part of every human relationship.

A YOUNG MOTHER who has just given birth says to all of this, "I probably wanted to keep the child to myself, didn't want to let it go." She asks herself whether this necessarily means she will have problems in later life letting the child become independent. Unprompted, she says she has problems anyway in letting go, difficulties when situations change. She says she prefers it when everything stays copacetic, stays familiar, and remains what she is used to. Is she holding on out of fear of the new, holding on out of lack of self-confidence?

Separation begins at birth. Yet once the child is born, the parents have to establish a relationship with it, so of course in this context, the pain of separation is less of an issue. What is of greater concern to everyone is the more or less frightening anticipation of a new life together. Still, there will be some mothers who do experience the post partum pain of separation.

Real separation, breaking away, is felt when the child takes its first independent steps. In a sense, this is the beginning of the end. While the pride parents feel about these first steps is combined with a slight melancholy, "a little stab in the heart," there is also a feeling of relief. Children's separation from us, their increasing independence, are simultaneous goals we strive towards. Our feelings are complex in the face of this process of becoming independent. While this is the normal course of events, the messages we send are quite often contradictory. We in fact encourage independent tendencies in our children, at least verbally, yet at the same time we restrict them. We do this by perhaps exaggerating the dangers which lurk in the world, and then pointing out the security which we think we offer.

Maybe we show all too clearly how painful it is to be alone, and in so doing, blackmail the children. "But mommy is sad when you go so far away," I recently heard a mother say to her approximately fifteen-month-old child, who was beaming as she toddled off into the world. The toddler kept glancing anxiously at her mother, yet nevertheless made it very clear that she still wanted to take her first steps out into the world. This child did not let herself be swayed by the words of her mother. She apparently understood them as being part of a game. The mother, feeling abandoned, waited until the child came back and then lovingly clasped her in her arms as though after a long separation.

The phrase, "Mommy is sad when you go away," can have far more problematic consequences than those described in the scenario above. During the course of a child's development, it can repeatedly give the child the feeling that separation is not allowed, that they may not develop in accordance with their age, that they may not seize life with open hands. The person who relates best to the child has an intense desire that the child not separate. In time this desire is internalized by the child. As a result, the child does not give itself permission to let go and subsequently turn to other people in the world. Such a life becomes increasingly restrictive. These children remain dependent too long, are too long not autonomous, not independent. They would like to walk headlong into the world, but feel that they may not. They stay, by analogy, standing on the threshold of the world and of other people. They cannot move forward, and yet they cannot really go back. Their desire to conquer is thwarted. They become fearful.[4]

If parents do not let go of their children, the children in turn have difficulty learning to let go. Yet there are very different responses between children and the people who relate to them best. Some parents actually provoke their children to cling to them. There are other parents who would not dream of holding on to their children beyond an appropriate age. When they do, it works counterproductively. Upbringing is not just something parents thrust on their children, something which the children simply put up with or are forced to accept. Every primary caregiver has a special relationship with a child. It is a harmony—sometimes discordant—and just like any other relationship, both parties either stimulate or inhibit one another in turn.

THE SEPARATION PROCESS takes place throughout childhood. There are also discernible signs of separation, turning-points at which it becomes clear that the quality of the relationship with the child is changing. These signs appear in the form of particular situations: the child enters a playgroup for the first time without looking around for the primary caregiver who brought her; the child goes to kindergarten and announces that he now wants to marry the kindergarten teacher and not mommy. The beginning of school, changing schools, and so on, are all signposts of separation which cannot be overlooked. In between these major events, there are many situations which make it clear that the child does not need us as much or in the same ways as before. The child is increasingly capable of shaping her own life and of doing more for herself. As a result, the parents become more independent again, and are consequently freed up for other life activities.

The separation phases proceed with a certain regularity. Children plunge into the world, they are proud of their independence. In so doing, they sometimes take on too much, become puzzled or frightened, then come back. This is the phase of reattachment[5] after separation. During this phase, even the most ambitious of children become weepy and cling to their mother's or father's apron-strings. They become quite babyish again. If they are lovingly picked up when they are like this and no one makes depreciating remarks about the unfortunate relapse into an earlier phase, then before long the so-called reattachment crisis occurs: the relationship, taken out of the context of the frightening experience, is too close, and leaves too little margin for possible autonomy. The child becomes whiny, aggressive, and becomes more independent again. In some children we can observe that the measure of independence is now somewhat corrected to a more acceptable level than existed before the first departure. The distance and the autonomy that have been gained balance one another out until new developmental steps introduce another "push for separation."

Separations in the life of human beings—also during adulthood—occur in cycles in which increasing capacity for autonomy is accompanied by a growing connectedness to the people with whom one lives.[6]

## Separation Phases Are
### Phases of Saying Goodbye

UNDERGOING EARLIER separation phases is important for making it through the separation phase of adolescence. Many problems parents have with children actually result from parental inability to let go of phases that have already passed.

A father says to his fifteen-year-old son, for example, "It was wonderful when you were ten or eleven and you hung on every word I said. I was really important to you. Why can't it stay like that? Why do you have to go through this difficult stage?" Having a fifteen-year-old son would be less difficult for the father, albeit difficult enough, if he had already let go of the idea that the relationship with his son would stay the same as the one he had with the ten- or eleven-year-old.

Saying goodbye is something that must be learned. The emotion which helps us to say goodbye and to process loss is grief. When we lose something that represents great value to us, we experience a loss and we are sad. Grief is the emotion which expresses the loss. At the same time, grief helps us to overcome the loss when we give ourselves over to the emotions that are intensified in the experience of "mourning." In the following chapter I will describe the mourning process in its various stages and show how it is manifest in people who have lost a loved one through death, which is an extreme experience of loss. In a second section, I will delineate how this mourning process—with some slight modifications—can be applied to the grief work that is necessary when we have to relinquish adult children to life.

# The Grieving Process

♦

WE ARE SEIZED BY A FEELING OF GRIEF when we lose a person or a thing that represents particular value to our life. This feeling of grief is accompanied by feelings of sorrow, of fear, rage, guilt, and so on.

By experiencing this feeling, by giving ourselves permission to feel, we enter into the grieving process. It is a process of development through which we slowly—and very painfully—learn to accept the loss and to open up to life again without the person or the thing that we have lost.

THE MOURNING PROCESS and the work of grieving must be seen in the context of the relationship from which we must free ourselves through loss. When we build up an intense relationship with a person, we grow together with that person, yet at the same time, we grow individually as well. This is why people in mourning say they feel as though they have been torn in two, that they feel like a bleeding wound, or as though they have been uprooted.

The process of this mutual growing together is abruptly interrupted by death and completely changes life. In the course of the mourning process we have to rethink ourselves as individuals and find an individual connection to the world. We have to reconstitute ourselves from a relationship-self back to our individual self. The loss concerns every aspect of life, particularly when it has to do with the loss of someone with whom we were very close.

The grieving process is a very painful process. It has a strange depth that demands enormous resources of strength and time. It compels us to take ourselves to task and to come into conflict with the relationship that has been broken off.

## The Different Phases

ONE CAN DESCRIBE a typical course of the mourning process by drawing on observations of people in mourning, and particularly by looking at the dreams that regularly accompany their grief.[7]

The first phase of the mourning process is what I call the phase of *disbelief*. One does not dare believe that the person is really dead. Living in a state of shock, initially the mourner tries to spare herself from the feelings of loss. She persuades herself that everything is just a bad dream from which she will awaken.

This first phase, which can last hours or days, gives way to the second phase, the *outbreak of chaotic emotions*. This phase often begins at the first sight of the corpse. That is when we can no longer repress the loss. These emotions are chaotic because the person feels various contradictory feelings such as sorrow, anger, rage, guilt, longing, love, and so on. Also included in this spectrum of feelings are periods of relative peacefulness, times of thankfulness, or even of joy.

During this phase, people frequently experience sleep disturbances and loss of appetite. There may also be an increased susceptibility to infection. The mourner is gripped by the feeling of having experienced an incisive loss, and by the inexorable impression that he or she has been separated from the world and from other people.

Very often, other people do not get along terribly well with the person who is in mourning. They are reminded that no life is immune to loss. Aside from that, a grieving person is not easily consoled. For this reason, he or she is given some cursory advice and instructed on just what they have to do in order to feel better.

For the person who goes through it, the grieving process is a lonely one. Yet people in mourning also make it difficult for those around them. They do not reach out to others, and they can also be very hard to get along with. Since what they really want is to have the dead person back, as a rule they just stop being obliging. For someone who is grieving there is a very clear differentiation between that which is crucial for existence and that which is of secondary importance—the person who is grieving cannot take the latter into consideration. Thus, the relationship is complicated by both parties, by those who are in mourning, and by those who want to give comfort. The best way to accompany a grieving person is to be there for them, to absorb the person's feelings, and to listen to the stories that he or she wants to tell. In addition, we can tell our own stories about experiences with the person who has died. In time, we can learn to absorb the feelings of the mourner without trying to make everything better. This means, however, that we have to withstand and accept the feelings of sorrow, fear, rage, and bewilderment in the other person, without wanting to change them. We have to listen to them without at the same time wanting to "console," so that we make ourselves feel better.

The anger which is generally experienced during this phase of the outbreak of chaotic emotions is manifested as rage at the world, at life, sometimes even at the dead person, or at God. This phase gives way to the phase of *searching, finding, and letting go.* Characteristic of this phase is that the person in mourning searches for the dead person in memories, in dreams, and in conversation with other people. The development of this process is initiated by the grieving person being very preoccupied by thoughts about the one who has died. "I can't think about anything other than the dead," is something one often hears from people in grief. This fixation is completely appropriate and is precisely what people should do to get themselves through this difficult time.

It is, after all, those who are left behind who have to

grieve. Their way of seeing themselves and their way of understanding the world have been shaken up. They sense that a fundamental change has taken place in their lives, a change that they did not seek. Because of this, mourners must be self-preoccupied in order to reconcile themselves to the new situation. Even when they are continually thinking about the person who has died, they are at the same time thinking about themselves, and about the relationship that existed between them.

During this recollection phase, the mourner is concerned with recalling the life story they shared with the person who has died. As long as a person with whom we are in a relationship is still alive, the relationship is ongoing. Having a vital relationship means we cannot instinctively reflect on the relationship to the same extent that we can once the person is dead. Then the relationship becomes fixed and immutable. We become aware that the relationship was important to us and that it has come to an end, at least in this world.

In undertaking this memory work, it is important to tell stories about the life we shared with the person who has died. By doing this, we not only reconstruct the common external and internal life we shared with the person, but are also forced to take back the projections we had. We have to find out to what extent we have burdened them with character traits of our own, to find out what we actually liked or disliked in them.

Retracting projections means, in other words, suddenly

recognizing that these character traits are really our own. The responsibilities we delegated away also have to be taken back: sides of ourselves that the person took care of or brought to life—things such as prestige in the eyes of the world, or filling out tax returns, perhaps—these prosaic things have to become our own responsibility again.

Of fundamental importance is that we work out which characteristics were stimulated in us by the person we have lost. Each person with whom we have a relationship is capable of addressing aspects of our personality that can only be awakened and stimulated by this particular person. In a love relationship there are typically deep, silenced sides of ourselves that are brought to life by the lover, aspects of our personalities that can be "loved out of us." Whatever has been animated, whether good or bad, by someone else, is something we do not have to give up for lost when we lose the relationship. It is also through these animated aspects of our personality that the dead live on in us and in our lives.[8]

During this phase, a mourner seeks and finds the dead person in myriad ways, not the least of which are dreams that convey to the mourner the impression that the dead person lives on in another form.

As Lewis formulates it, death is a phenomenon that has to be reckoned with.[9] The dead person is an entity that continues to affect our lives in discernable ways, a reality that cannot and may not be transcended.

The mourner tries to conjure up sense memories by

evoking images of the dead person. These images acquire a strange significance and lead to a new relationship with someone who is no longer part of the concrete everyday world, and with whom this everyday existence can only be shared in a very curtailed manner.

At the beginning of this phase, the dead person is often idealized and the relationship with him or her is very harmonious. However, this harmony can seldom be maintained for any great length of time; over and over again, everyday life reinforces awareness of the person's merciless absence, their painful absence in daily life. Sexual needs, and needs for affection, remind one of the person who is no longer around. In these moments, the experience of loss becomes unbearable again and the mourner is resubmerged in chaotic feelings. The phases are repeated, and we have to get through them all over again. Whenever the feeling of loss predominates, mourners find themselves in the phase I call the outbreak of chaotic emotions. In time—and this proves that the symbol of the spiral is also applicable to this psychic process—one realizes that this phase of doubt and abandonment will also come to an end, and that a phase of relative well-being will begin.

It is precisely through this process of continually re-experiencing the feelings of loss, which correspond to the concrete loss, that the inner relationship to the dead person can change. As a result, one's own inner image of the dead person changes, too.

The dead person is not lost through this process. In an inexorable way the dead belong to the life of the mourner. The only difference is that the mourner turns toward life again, and where possible, reengages in new relationships.

The loss has now been accepted. The pain over the death can now be sacrificed, as indeed it must be. Sometimes it seems that pain has taken the place of the person who has died. People may think that sacrificing the pain means forgetting the person who has died. However, the pain has to be sacrificed, and in so doing one does not sacrifice the relationship with the person. Instead, one releases the relationship into an ever-changing form and, simultaneously, sets oneself free for perpetual development.

Having accomplished this step, we are able to see ourselves as persons who have indeed suffered a great loss, and yet at the same time as someone who can be "whole" for him- or herself again. Friends who appear, new ideas, and so on, can all be enjoyed. They do not need to be made victim to perpetual pain. Memories of life with the person who has died will always resurface, yet at the same time they also belong to this new way of life. The memory just does not govern one's whole life, as it once did. We experience feelings of gratitude for the distance that we covered together, and for the aspects of ourself that the person brought to life. Sometimes we also feel a certain regret that too little was made of the relationship, that we postponed too much for a later date, that certain things can now never be.

Relationships become costly for people who have suffered a loss. If a person who has suffered a loss that has been mourned should subsequently enter into a new relationship, then they can only do so with conflicting emotions: They will want to get totally involved with another person, yet know that relationships can come to an end. There is the fear of allowing oneself to get completely involved, when one now knows the price of the potential feelings of loss and the times of grief.

Undergoing a mourning process affords one the possibility of feeling more secure again. One's sense of oneself and one's own feelings of self-worth also restabilize. It is to be remembered that unless it is in some way inhibited, the grieving process is a process that runs its own spontaneous course in every human being.

### The Difference between
### Grief and Depression

THE GRIEF RESPONSE to loss is distinct from that of a depressive reaction. At a psychomotor level, symptoms such as impeded mobility and a sense of inertia seem common to both the grieving process and to depression; similarly, the symptoms at a psychosomatic level. Both phenomena can induce sleep disturbances, lack of appetite, and the absence of sexual drive. Also in evidence may be dizziness, pressure in the chest, a "lump in the throat," and generally diffuse ailments. However, the symptoms of grief and depression can be differentiated at a psychic and a psychosocial level. With depression, sufferers experience an "emptiness" that is associated with the loss of feelings or with a defense against feelings, particularly aggression. The absence of feelings is manifest as an emptiness. With people who are grieving, however, the emptiness or absence of feelings is but short-lived. It is rapidly followed by chaotic emotions which make the mourner feel very much alive.

The mourning process also differs in that people express aggression. With depression, people's thoughts are always centered on the feelings of emptiness. One is, so to speak, worried about the worry. Self-reproach and self-depreciation or devaluing the world play a large role. In the mourning process, thoughts center on the person who has been lost, and on oneself, the person who has been left behind. Consequently, the mourner does not feel useless and rejected by the world, as does the depressive person. By withdrawing from the world, the mourner retreats in order to take stock of the self. He or she will also reemerge and turn to the world again. Thus, the fundamental problem in the depressive reaction, the degrading self-loathing, the devaluing of the world, and the search for scapegoats, is clearly different from the basic problem in the grief reaction. The latter comprises a shaking-up of the established identity and, consequently, the search for a new identity.

If the emotions of grief are warded off—above all, those that emerge during the phase of chaotic emotions—

then a depression can ensue. When this happens, we stave off and repress all the feelings that cause pain: powerful aggression and fear, for example. We also repress the feelings that are not easy to reconcile with our usual self-image. Repressing these emotions diminishes one's capacity for activity, enthusiasm for life, and one's feelings of genuineness. Self-respect wanes. A circle of retreat is established. This precludes the possibility of processing either the loss or the illness that is associated with the loss. The aggression which is not expressed turns against the self. This releases yet more fear, which in certain cases leads to self-destructive impulses. The fear and the self-destructive impulses must themselves be repressed, and so one maneuvers oneself into an ever-downward spiral.

AS I HAVE suggested above, averted grief is most likely to lead to depression when someone avoids the second phase of the grieving process and its outbreak of chaotic emotions. This sort of repression often occurs because the mourner is reluctant to be unduly burdensome to the people around them. Of course it also has to do with the fact that in our culture one is seen as being virtuous if one can be a "man," and pull oneself together, even if it would be better for our health to release these emotions and express them fully. In today's world, expressing emotions demands at the very least that we be courageous.

Depression readily appears as a reaction to loss when the person we have lost was the one who guaranteed our own self-worth. This is particularly true when, instead of generating our own feelings of natural self-value, we draw our only source of worth from the person with whom we had a relationship. People whose self-worth comes almost exclusively from their partner's esteem often have an innately depressive personality structure. Having a depressive personality structure does not necessarily mean being depressed. It just means that the likelihood of responding to loss or serious illness with depression is greater in these people than in others. People with a depressive personality structure have learned early in life to adapt themselves to the desires of the people around them. In other words, they have an overdeveloped capacity to conform, and consequently sacrifice their own wishes and their own life plans.

The unconscious expectation is this: If I do what other people want, then I will be loved. However, the reality is that people who adapt themselves, who do everything in order to be loved a little, lend themselves to being exploited. We can make use of them for our own purposes, we can exploit them. But we are unlikely to love them for this quality. At best, they may be appreciated. Loving feelings have a deeper basis. For a person who is unconscious of their depressive structure, the world takes on an ever more demanding character: one is surrounded by demands, by requirements which cannot be satisfied, yet which one must honor. If people with a depressive personality structure sense that although they are doing everything in their power—or perhaps even more than that—to be loved and yet no love is forthcoming, then they too will become angry with the people around them. However, they cannot allow themselves to stay angry, since they fear the loss of the little bit of love that they mean to keep. Instead, they turn the rage against themselves and tell themselves, "If I were to sacrifice myself even more, then perhaps I really would be loved."

These feelings of guilt, linked with aggression directed against the self, are the corollary of a hidden self-depreciation and a secret depreciation of other people. Their real guilt lies in the fact that these people take too little responsibility for their own self-being. They pay too little attention to the call to be themselves. Even when they act completely "selflessly" and say that their actions are quite selfless, when they function according to the motto, "everything for others, and nothing for myself," then this may to some extent be true. On the other hand, it is not true. Life simply cannot tolerate so much selflessness. The flip-side of selflessness is that people may be very demanding. There exists, for example, a lifelong unspoken assumption on the part of the depressive, that people who help maintain the sense of self-worth will stick around. Alternatively, they may express an indisputable demand for a particular kind of behavior that is supposed to perpetuate a certain quality of life.

If we are so selfless, then what is missing is our own "self." The grieving process demands that we rethink ourselves. We have to shift from a relationship-self to an individual-self, and in so doing, also assume a new definition of our identity. However, if we cannot retreat back to our individual-self then we become depressive. The opportunity that this depressive reaction affords is that we may be able to find our own self through a therapeutic process, that we will become autonomous and in touch with our own depths.

It seems to me that socialization requires women to develop a depressive personality structure. First and foremost, women learn (or used to learn?) to find themselves loveable in the mirror of other people, particularly men, of course. Women are less loveable in their own eyes, unpracticed at regarding themselves in calm, critical self-acceptance. Women make themselves far too dependent upon the reactions of the world around them, and are taught to read other people's desires in their eyes in order to be valued by the world. All around us there are subliminal images of women which are fatal to our own sense of well-being, images of which we are too little aware, and whose effect on relationships is too little questioned. If people glean their measure of self-worth from external sources instead of constructing it themselves, drawing it from their own vitality, from their power to act and shape things, from the power of eros, and so on, then people become manipulable. Instead of demanding an equal voice and actively shaping relationships and life itself, they just react.

A depressive personality structure is sometimes represented as an almost "female" characteristic, or at any rate as something thoroughly central and practical in the everyday coexistence of the family. This attitude prevails in spite of the fact that it is extremely unhealthy for those who have and live with such a personality type. Thus, it is no wonder that it is more frequently women who react with depression to separation from grown children, and to the problems associated with separation.

# Grieving in the Separation Process—A Phase of Life Comes to an End

◆

ASSUMING THAT THE GRIEVING PROCESS can take place, and that we can in fact reconstitute ourselves as independent selves, I will proceed to show the most important ways in which the grieving process is modified in the separation process.

When we lose a person who was close to us through death or divorce, the grieving process that we have to undergo differs from the grieving process that takes place in the event of a separation. In the mourning process associated with separation, we might find ourselves stuck in the phase of not wanting to believe for a lot longer. When this happens we simply pretend to ourselves that nothing has really changed. Sentences such as, "She has moved out of course, but she is still with us all the time. Actually things are pretty much the same," can indicate that the profound change or, as the case may be, the minor changes in the family dynamic, have been repressed rather than accepted.

Separation-induced grieving differs from other types of grieving. With separation-induced grieving, people do not rail against the outside world to the same extent whilst going through the phase of chaotic emotions. However, this can be deceptive: Parents often harbor a grudge against their children's friends. Parents see the friends as having "spoiled" their children, or as having encouraged them to move out. Friends who simply love the child may, for example, be characterized as having "taken advantage" of them. Whatever the case, parents see the child's friends as having committed the sin of alienating the child from the parents. Many problems between in-laws are in actual fact due to projected anger and projected pain: we cannot stand feeling angry that these children, for whom we have done so much, simply leave. We cannot bear it that someone else could be so much more important in their lives. So we free ourselves from this rage by finding something wrong with the new significant other. Finding something wrong with them allows us to justify the anger.

Parents' emotions towards their children can also be decidedly chaotic: we are not interested in them, are angry with them, yet at the same time sense that we love them just as we did before. We thrive when they reappear.

Yet we do not speak much about these feelings. Parents who find themselves engaged in this separation phase are also not encouraged to speak about their feelings. Even if they have a close relationship, parents sometimes conceal the way they feel not only from other people but also from one another. Alternatively, the conflict with grief might be blocked according to an established pattern. One of the parents expresses the feelings; they might even be very articulate about what they are going through. The other parent tries to comfort, to prove that this is the normal course of life, that there is no reason to act so "unreasonably." It is normal that children leave their parents. Yet even though it is normal, this does not mean that it might not hurt and that the pain may not and ought not be expressed.

Guilt feelings also play a big role in grieving processes that are associated with separation. It is not just a case of adolescents eliciting guilt feelings from the parents. Because adolescents are leaving their parents and actually feel guilty themselves, adolescents project their sense of guilt onto their parents in an effort to ward off their own feelings. As a result, the parents become scapegoats, and in fact often behave as such. At the same time, it is also an issue of the secret guilt feelings harbored by the parents. They know that they owe their individual children different things, debts that have accumulated over the years just by virtue of being a human being. It can be helpful if these secret guilt feelings (which may correspond to actual wrong-doing) are taken seriously and accepted. If not, feelings of guilt can easily seduce parents into trying valiantly, but unsuccessfully, to "make good," frequently at an inappropriate time and place. Alternatively, we might look for our own scapegoats in order to free ourselves from the unpleasant guilt feelings. And sometimes, we coddle specific guilt feelings expressly so that we do not have to examine our true guilt and the ways in which we perpetuate wrong-doing.

IN CONNECTION WITH the third phase of grieving, the phase of searching, finding, and letting go, it has been established that many parents think about their children a lot, frequently with great concern. With separation-induced grieving it is at least possible for everyone concerned to deal with what has transpired. Parents and children can give one another the opportunity to work out common problems. This is not, however, the case when one mourns someone who has died: problems in the relationship exist in perpetuity. In an ongoing relationship, problems can at least be attended to and perhaps even avoided. Yet we frequently suffer in silence without all this worrying changing anything. This sort of apprehension is just a disguised form of the doubt we feel about the adolescent's potential for independence. It functions in a downright destructive manner, and is justifiably rejected by young people. The appropriate response that we need to strive for is a balance between real letting-go, which is based on trust in the capabilities and potential of the young person, and a concerned interest that is not obtrusive, but which nevertheless makes it clear that one is still available, and that one cares about how the child's future shapes up.

Our own idealizations also emerge during this phase. We cover up feelings of rage about the loss, as well as the guilt that we feel. We also pretend to ourselves that we have brought up the most perfect children in the world. Quite often, in building up our child, we also undercut the child's partner. If children are excessively idealized—a milder form seems to be symptomatic of all parents— then children have the feeling that they are not really taken seriously by their parents, and the separation process can easily come to a standstill.

Only seldom do parents do any memory work. Seldom do we think about the life with the child in order to reexperience the qualities the child evoked in us through the years. We do not reflect on the qualities that must not be given up for lost, that live on in us, even when the child, or rather the adolescent, no longer lives with us. Doing this sort of memory work would be far easier if we were aware early on that it would one day need to be done. If we did not just wait until the last minute, we could talk to the child on an ongoing basis about the qualities that the child brings to life in us. This memory work could even take the form of a common ritual: From time to time we might sit down together and reflect on the qualities we evoke in each other, the good things and the bad. This could be seen as a preliminary exercise to prepare for the time when parents and child really say goodbye, for a time when the child's presence no longer constantly evokes something, simply because the child is not around all the time.

Every child awakens very special sides in us, good sides and bad ones: these qualities can only be evoked in the relationship, and through the relationship with this very special child—they are precious. Besides this, children, in certain phases of their lives, evoke specific qualities which are comparable. Basically, they stimulate the childlike in us and the respective motherly or fatherly characteristics. Thus, in most people, the infant elicits tenderness, a tendency to protect, and to convey security. Feelings of merging with the little one also come to the fore, feelings of symbiosis, of the eternal. We are imbued with a sense of complete connectedness. These feelings are associated with great trust.

Yet when the child becomes more independent, we lose these feelings of merging with the little one that has entrusted itself to us. We do not, however, erase the feelings from our consciousness. They are feelings we can remember.

Through the years, there are other aspects of feeling childlike that are evoked through a shared life with the child. What thirty-five-year-old would, for example, sit in a sandbox and play without a care in the world? A smaller child gives us the opportunity to completely liberate this childlike element in ourselves. It is not only small children who like to play in the most carefree way in the sandbox. It is often the parents who play gleefully with cars, trains, and scores of dolls.

School children, with their myriad interests, enable us to go to primary school all over again, and to learn something new in the process. School children also introduce new role models into the family, something that parents are often jealous of. That children find other people appealing has nothing to do with whether or not children are still completely dependent on their parents. It has to do with the fact that children can also love other people, which merely confirms that the child is capable of love. And of course everyone wants to raise children who have the capacity to love other people. So what about our jealousy then? Is the problem, perhaps, that we just cannot let go?

Most primary caregivers enjoy the qualities evoked in them by a child until the child is about twelve years of age. Up until this point, we have the opportunity to make up for what we missed as a child, to recapture the child in ourselves. The child evokes qualities like creativity, movement, self-abandon, and a certain openness to new things. If we let ourselves be challenged by our children, they can introduce many new impulses into family life. During the next stage of development, however, pubescents also awaken the pubescent in the primary caregiver. Now all of a sudden, parents find it difficult to see the situation as being stimulating, even though it most certainly is. Consider the way adolescents will often bring home music that one doesn't know and that one perhaps mistrusts; they bring home world-views that one regards with great skepticism. The very things one has tried to avoid in life, are just what the teenager finds so attractive.

The great separation that occurs during adolescence takes place when teenagers express aspects of the parents that have been suppressed in the family system, qualities that do not concur with the conscious and explicit family values. Adolescents express the shadows of the family system and give voice to whatever opposes the ideal that the family has made for itself. In so doing, adolescents find it possible to separate from the parents, although their separation is never as great as the parents fear and the children hope for. The shadows are still part of the family system. Furthermore, the qualities that children evoke during this phase are the very ones that the parents have fended off all their lives. In actual fact, this would be a wonderful opportunity for us to learn more about ourselves, to become conscious of what we have experienced and what we have repressed. It could also be an opportunity to consider whether certain convictions that we hold aren't perhaps too narrow. We could also try to let go of our own self-deceptions. Finally, we could consider whether we have not perhaps renounced too much in the name of an ideal, something which we now envy in other people, particularly our own children.

During this phase, it takes a lot of honesty and self-awareness to summon up gratitude for what the adolescents evoke in us, and ultimately even gratitude for the upset they cause to the family system. For the most part, however, we make little attempt at understanding; instead, there is fighting and jealousy. Naturally we won't confess to feeling envious. We do not want to admit that we are envious of young people who risk more than we risked. We do not want to acknowledge that we envy their appearance, their opportunities in relationships, or the fact that this day and age is perhaps more conducive to relationships. We may also feel a clandestine, tenacious jealousy over the way they allow themselves to do things that are fun, things that we have given up in the name of some ideal or other. Very often we can no longer even say with certainty whether it really is an ideal worth upholding or not. Naturally we do not own our feelings of jealousy. Instead, we devalue the person who evokes the feelings of envy, we criticize them.

However, it is not only the parents' shadows that come into play during separation. Also brought to life are the archetypal images which constitute the basis of the mother and father-complexes.[11] One can see this manifest, for example, in an adolescent's increased interest in religion. The adolescent's interest may focus on various different godlike figures. In conjunction with this religious preoccupation, or in place of it, teenagers may show a marked political interest. In fact, these preoccupations show that the individual feels as though they are an integral part of society. They create a support structure for the maturing person who is leaving the family. To a certain extent, they replace the mother and father. Just as in the case of the "shadow" life of the parents, the adolescent compensates for what was missing when he or she was growing up. Images of God, political and philosophical ideas, and so on, are not just those transmitted by the parents: they are often ideas that are exact polar opposites of the values the parents have tried to imbue in their children. In other words, this is a stage of development that dispenses with onesidedness. Parents obviously don't see this development in a terribly positive light. It is more likely that they will feel as though the values that they have conveyed to their children are not heeded and do not carry any weight. It is the value-conscious parents, in particular, who suffer from the painful sense of a devaluation of their own values.

A PHASE OF LIFE quite clearly comes to an end here. Lots of criticism and a great many power struggles ensue simply because we do not want to acknowledge that a phase of life is coming to an end and that we have to mourn its passing. Primary caregivers and adolescents who are separating from them have to grieve, even though it is just a matter of the children going out into the world. The whole of life lies before the children, while the parents, even if not exactly old, are at least middle-aged and have to remain behind. Even if they are in their best years, it is clear that they have had their heyday. This can be yet another cause for envy, if the parents do not consent to a graceful passing into old age, into their new phase of life.

During this phase, young people learn separation behavior. In teaching separation behavior, the grief work can be instituted as though of its own accord. We can reexplore the past in everyday conversation when young people ask about their early childhood; we can reiterate the qualities that the other person evokes, we can talk about what is left behind and cannot be lost, what was lacking, what was difficult—certainly not all at once, but over and over again.

The fourth phase of the grieving process has quite a distinct character when it comes to the separation process. The son or daughter from whom we have separated does not disappear out of our life altogether—but our relationship with them is nevertheless fundamentally different. There is a great danger in wanting to make the whole separation process "regress," since both parties have the tendency to repeatedly fall back into old, long-practiced positions and ways of behaving. This phase, which lasts an entire lifetime, is characterized by a search for "appropriate" closeness and at the same time, "appropriate" distance. "Appropriate" closeness and distance is not something that we can once and for all grasp and then apply. It is something that has to be flexible and must correspond to each participant's psychological needs for intimacy and autonomy. It has to do with a very differentiated relationship process which works best if we accept and respect the autonomy of all the participants. By respecting these boundaries we learn to "read" the signs for more or less contact, more or less connection. As a result, the concrete behavior within the relationship becomes a compromise between the needs of all parties. However, if the needs for autonomy are not heeded, and should one of the participants deny the separation, then the only alternatives are either an open or a secret escape. Denying autonomy and the need for separation can, for example, result in parents and children still maintaining the original family constellation, even long after it has become passé. Should this happen, the children may withdraw by secretly escaping into illness or perhaps into a fantasy life that can never be realized. They undergo an inner emigration.[12]

# How Adolescents Separate from Their Parents

◆

THE SEPARATION BEHAVIOR OF ADOLESCENTS is dependent upon many factors: Young people who have completed their age-appropriate stages of separation, and are as a result secure in their identities, will find it easier to separate than those who have always been held back or who have held themselves back. Another factor that influences separation is the family motto that all families have. Specific mottos say a lot about family cohesion and, by extension, about the boundaries that are allowed in the family. One family motto might say, for example, "Become independent quickly." Such families permit a lot of separation. However, under certain circumstances, they offer little protection if for some reason a child cannot or does not want to become independent. On the other hand, other families have a secret command that says, "We never want to be apart." Also influential in determining the separation behavior of the adolescent is the type of partner relationship that the parents have. If, for example, one parent has to be protected from the other one, then a child cannot really "go." Social values play a role as well. Whether it is currently "in" to become independent early or, alternatively, living at a time when it is in vogue to make use of the family infrastructure for as long as possible, are all factors which influence separation behavior. Naturally parents who let themselves be exploited and parents who cannot separate are also part of the equation.

The process of separation is complicated. Among other reasons, it is difficult because in order to enter into a new relationship—not as children, which we of course remain, but as adults—we do not just have to separate from our actual parents. We also have to intrapsychically separate from our parent-complexes. Our parent-complexes, the mother- and father-complexes, develop out of our lives with our parents. The father and mother, with their wishes, demands, points of view, and so on, always come into conflict with the desires of the child's ego.[13] The point at which we always clash, where there is continual conflict, is where "complexes" develop, generally called "father- or mother-complexes." Father- and mother-complexes are particularly evident in situations involving illness and difficult relationships.

A STUDENT WITH a severe work disorder recalls that for almost as long as he can remember (at least since he was aged five) his father was always hypercritical of the things he had made. His father would scrutinize a drawing, for example, and typically say, "One mustn't just like doing something, one also has to be able to do it." This sentence repeated "millions of times" during the course of a lifetime developed into a complex. Now, if the son sits with a blank piece of paper and cannot think of something straight away, then he hears his father saying to him, "One mustn't just like doing it, one also has to be able to do it." And in his conscious mind he is like a disappointed five-year-old lad who feels as though he has made his father angry for some reason. The son feels insecure, fearful, and in need of continually justifying why he still has the piece of paper in front of him. A whole slew of emotions comes up.

The separation from our parental complexes is part and parcel of the separation from our parents, albeit a more unconscious process during adolescence. Even so, many reproaches which children make against parents have less to do with the parents *per se,* and with what they are really like during this phase, than with these parental complexes. Parents are often surprised and pained that the children do not take their reality seriously, and that the children do not recognize their parents as independently existing people with their own capabilities, worries, and needs. Parents often feel that even grown children only perceive them as having certain characteristics. Parents may be able to fully recognize this problematic trait and the extent to which it affects the children's perceptions, but nevertheless know that they are not as limited as the children make them out to be. On the other hand, it is also important for parents to actually hear the reproaches mounted by the children, since the criticism could be an impetus for possible change. Parents should not, however, just whole-heartedly identify with these reproaches. Children do not see the totality of their parents, and even when complexes are consciously identified over the course of a lifetime, parental complexes are always the easiest to project. For the most part, parents are always available and do not change their spots, so it is easy to get the impression that one's projections have hit the mark. Sometimes it is only through therapy that we are shown how old relationship problems are being restaged, even though we are no longer children, and father and mother are also no longer the people they once were.

The relationship between parents and children is a relationship of continual detachment. We can liken this process to the image of an onion: the outer layer is removed over and over again leaving the impression that we have finally separated, and then we notice that new phases of separation keep appearing and have to be taken into consideration. At the same time, we ought not forget that parents are also engaged in separation processes with their own parents. In all likelihood, they are probably influenced by the same kind of separation behavior as their children, who are also just detaching.

Nevertheless, the separation phase in adolescence is obviously a particularly decisive one. From this separation phase follow enormous consequences for a person's social life: the first apartment, a family of one's own, and so on.

# The Avoided Separation

♦

## Gerda: An Example

A FORTY-EIGHT-YEAR-OLD WOMAN, whom I will call
Gerda, comes to therapy. She complains that she feels no
joy in life any more, that the many responsibilities that
she has to fulfill are burdensome to her, and are actually
becoming overwhelming. Everything is too much, and "everyone else" is to blame. By this she means that, objec-
tively speaking, she can manage far less work than ever
before. She also perpetually suffers from some infection
or other, albeit minor afflictions, and also from insomnia.
She has become a regular burden to herself. "I have really
had enough of myself, I must be terrible for my family as
well." She has no interest in sex any more and is increasingly plagued by the thought that this might cause her
husband to go in search of a girlfriend. Gerda is a housewife, and was with all her heart and soul a mother. She
has three children who have all left home, the youngest

son two years ago. She had hoped that he would stay at home longer—after all, they have such a nice, big house. Friends had seduced him into living in a share; things happen there in a less orderly fashion than at home. Occasionally, he lets her tidy up his things and cook his favorite meal. Actually it bothers her that he only comes home when it suits him. All the children still have a key to their parents' house; they, on the other hand, have no keys to the children's new apartments. Particularly the youngest "uses her for all manner of things." "But what one won't do in order to see one's children again."

Gerda seems angry when she tells the story, but does not sense her own anger. She feels old, and knows that the relationship with her husband could be important now. He, on the other hand, has buried himself in all kinds of responsibilities and demands; she sees him less than ever before.

Everything is not what it once was, and there is no alternative in sight. The children are not exactly in a hurry to get married, so that for the moment, there won't be any grandchildren for her to take care of either. Gerda says that today's world, this state of affairs, not to mention women who want to acquire a profession, is what's to blame for it all. Her point of view is drawn from her own life experience, specifically the fact that she never learned a skill. As a result, she now feels somewhat "useless" in contemporary society. It pains Gerda that the children have a lifestyle that is so opposed to her own. "I have done so much for my children, I raised them so carefully, and now they behave as though they hadn't had a decent upbringing." It also grieves her that the children criticize their parents, her husband as well as herself. In fact, they are even more critical of him.

Her feelings culminate in the realization that she took great pains to do everything possible for her children—her children were at the center of her life—and now, apart from criticism, there is "nothing coming back" in return. And sometimes she even senses that her children feel a certain contempt for her and her "bourgeois lifestyle." "You two can't do anything other than work, you don't know how to live"—that is one of the frequently reiterated criticisms that she and her husband hear from their children.

GERDA SUFFERS BECAUSE her husband does indeed see these problems, but he thinks that it is just a normal phase that one has to go through. She does not feel as though she is understood by anyone, neither by the children, nor by her husband. Gerda suffers from a typical "empty-nest" depression: her whole life was oriented towards the upbringing of her children and towards family life; now that the "nest" is empty, she feels a sense of emptiness, yet doesn't know what she should do with herself. She sees no meaning in life anymore, and has slowly come to feel that she has always done everything for everyone else but never done anything for herself.

She thinks she really ought to be getting something in

return now. She would be prepared to continue fulfilling the demands of her children, just so she did not have to face up to the fact that a phase of life has come to an end. She does not want to acknowledge that she must separate from this phase and from the children, and that she has to find a new life-plan of her own that will see her through the remainder of her life.

She asks herself whether her ill-humor might not have something to do with menopause. Her husband suggests this diagnosis to her, and friends of hers have also made hints in this direction. In other words, a menopausal depression—a popular, but questionable diagnosis. Even so, menopause does frequently coincide with the final separation from the children.

## The Process of Change

THE FIRST ISSUE that Gerda deals with in the context of a deep psychology-oriented psychotherapy is menopause. She says that the reason she feels so fearful, so dissatisfied, probably has something to do with menopause. She wonders whether there was any point in having had a family, and whether her husband is a suitable partner for her: "Sometimes I think that couldn't possibly have been all there was to life."

Even though she doesn't yet feel any menopausal changes, it is possible that she could be in the pre-menopausal phase. It would not worry her as much if she could be reassured that it was just the hormonal changes in her body that were responsible for the feelings of meaninglessness and the depressive ill-humor. The "experts" do more or less offer her this explanation. I try to explain to her that a major life transition is of course due, that hormonal changes are occurring in her body, but that various different explanations would also be in order. Her malaise could be attributed to her new identity as a woman now that her mothering role has finally played itself out; the question of age ought to be taken into consideration; also the question of what she should do for the rest of her life; and not to mention the concrete leave-taking from the children.

GERDA IS AFRAID of becoming old. She sees no difference between menopause and extreme old age, in which her almost eighty-year-old mother now finds herself. She formulates this idea several times, "By the time menopause is over, I will be very old." When asked about what "very old" might imply in her case, she says that it means having virtually no interest in life any more, not being sexually attractive, and also not being interested in sex any more. "No one will pay any attention to me—everything will simply be over."

In speaking about menopause, it becomes abundantly clear to what extent Gerda has drawn her identity and value as a woman from sexual attraction and fertility. It is also clear that she is trapped by the erroneous assumption that sexuality ends with menopause. However, the really frightening thing for her is that she cannot even remotely imagine continuing to be an attractive woman.

Gerda dreamed repeatedly about attractive older women she was acquainted with, women who both fascinated and frightened her because they all lived less conventional lifestyles than she. After making contact with some of these women and speaking with them about how they had experienced menopause, her expectations changed somewhat. In fact, she became totally appreciative of the fact that all these women had deliberately and carefully planned the next phase of life. Each in their own way, these women now tried to make up for whatever it was that they had missed in life. Gerda realized that none of these women felt worthless, nor did they let themselves be defined by a purely biological existence. This was how we tackled the topic of menopause for the first time.

In therapy, it became clear that Gerda still frequently quoted her parents. She represented herself as being the "good daughter," and gave the impression that she had not really separated from her still living parents. She repeatedly expressed feelings of gratitude to her parents for all they had given her. She visited her parents often, even when she didn't feel like it, and despite the fact that her parents are still active and proud and are capable of taking care of their own household. At the beginning of therapy, Gerda discussed many other problems she had with her parents.

Without her having to mention any further details, it became clear that Gerda had never completed the age-appropriate stages of separation. She seemed to be still very tied to her parents. This suggested to me that the family motto in her family of origin must have been: "We never want to be apart." Her original family cultivates a close unity; autonomy is little valued.

This woman, who has not really separated from her own parents and her original family, is now having great difficulty letting her children become independent. She recalls that it caused her a lot of pain even when the children were little, when they first began to shout "myself, myself," and took enormous delight in being able to hide from her. Later on, she was actually glad that she had children who were rather fearful, and who needed her more than other less fearful children needed their mothers. What she did not see was that the fearfulness of her children actually had something to do with her own fears about separation.

IN THE FIRST PHASES of therapy, Gerda became aware of the extent to which her life had changed. Pain and rage about the departure of the children came to the surface. She also felt angry about the unabashed demands which they still placed on her and which she fulfilled in a downright servile way. Her pain also had to do with the loss of her role as a mother, the role which had unquestionably justified her existence. Up until now, she had never really asked herself whether or not she was a "real woman," whether her life had meaning—it had all been taken as a matter of course—and now these very issues were not being taken for granted anymore. In the meantime, it was clear to her that a new role had to be found. But which one?

In this regard, she also began to question her role as the obedient daughter, a role she had always assumed. It became painfully clear to her how much she had ruled out just because it would have given her parents cause for worry. The fantasy of a life less burdened by parents would in time become very important. In conjunction with these fantasies came new life choices, which could at least in part still be realized.

But it wasn't just her stifled fantasies that she became aware of. She also became angry that her parents were so opposed to any modicum of autonomy, and that they had not supported her efforts to break away. Yet by the same token, she also remained thankful to them for the fact that they had not actively hindered her in life, and had always given her a loving, secure home.

GRATITUDE WAS an important topic for her. Indeed, she could now appreciate that her children, by more or less fleeing home and living so differently from their parents— and from their grandparents, who also did not condone their lifestyle—had completed, or at least taken important preliminary steps towards separating. Sometimes it gave her satisfaction that her children were clearly stronger than she had been at a comparable age. Yet at the same time, she still unyieldingly and tenaciously demanded that the children be grateful. I tried to work with her to establish what qualities the children had already evoked in her during the course of life together. In other words, I wanted to find out what they had already "given" her. In so doing, I wanted to make it clear that as a mother, one doesn't simply give things to children, things that they in turn have to give back when they are older. In reality, the giving is always accompanied by a receiving. And grown children do not first and foremost have to "give something back." The life-force that one invests in the relationship with one's children cannot and may not be given back by them. It is just a natural part of life that every generation takes care of the next generation, that it reinvests all the love, solicitousness, and energy that was once invested in it. Aside from all Gerda's cares and worries, she soon recalled how much fun her children had brought into her life. Gerda was well aware of all the qualities the children had awakened in her, each child in its own way. She could speak at length about how her son, already by the age of five, had enabled her to be more courageous in swimming. Her other son had suddenly begun to collect sentimental songs with a passion. At first she had tried to spoil the songs for him—it really wasn't the right sort of thing for a boy. She made fun of his "sentimental vein," yet one evening her son had coerced her into singing all the songs with him. She felt that as a result, an emotive quality came into her life, one that she had simply rejected since her own adolescence. She felt wonderfully alive. Memory work such as this allows one to remember more and more things, if one will just allow some of the memories to really come alive. Gerda tried to carry on this memory work in family life. Her husband also let himself be prompted to remember, and when one of the children was home visiting, the child was likewise included in the conversation.

Gerda knew which of the traits evoked by her children reawakened issues that could be dangerous for her. Her daughter's "intellectual affectation," for example, was a thorn in her flesh. The daughter had attended high school and then gone on to college. She did this all in a self-evident, rather casual way, and besides this, she had lots of hobbies, she passionately loved to cook, and was interested in breeding dogs. She presumably kept a check on the "intellectual affectation," but her mother nevertheless experienced it as such. On the one hand, her daughter's course of life aroused Gerda's own desire to study. Initially, she expressed a great interest in her daughter's field. Later on, however, she put it down more and more, together with all women who "sit around studying." Gerda was jealous, consumed by a gnawing envy. She would also have liked to know more, but how was she supposed to go about it? She didn't think she would still be able to take the final high school examinations she needed to get into college. Naturally, she did not admit that she felt envious. Instead she turned it into a binding ideology: "Women who study are not real women." Her daughter didn't know how anyone in today's world could hold such old-fashioned views. She wondered what was wrong with her mother.

In general, envy made it difficult for Gerda to function, as far as her daughter was concerned. It did not escape Gerda's notice that their daughter was the apple of her husband's eye. He also made observations to the effect that his daughter reminded him of her when she was eighteen, and he had just met her. He probably meant it kindly, but Gerda thought it was an unfair comparison: your daughter is young and pretty; you, on the other hand, are slowly becoming old and silly. Had she asked her husband whether he had really intended to imply this message in his observation, she would most certainly have saved herself a lot of worry. Of course she wanted her daughter to have the good things in life, to have a better deal than she had, but must her daughter outshine her in everything? Gerda would catch herself in the act of starting to criticize her daughter; she couldn't find anything right about her anymore. This hypercriticism of her daughter caused Gerda anguish all over again, and resulted in the fact that the daughter became even more attached to her father—something she had been inclined to do throughout her life anyway. Gerda had heard from friends that daughters could also be trusted friends, and Gerda saw that she was once again getting the worst of it. However, the thing that aroused the most envy was the ease with which her daughter could study. Gerda silently began to reproach her own parents for their views: when she was little they had conveyed the idea that since girls marry and just have children, there was no need for her to learn anything. She knew, of course, that at the time she had been only too willing to buy into that line of argument. She also knew that back then her parents didn't know any better. Even so, she remembered that she had had girlfriends who had learned a skill, some of them even going against their parents' wishes in order to do so. These women friends were not more talented than she was, but perhaps they had just been less fearful.

By questioning her own life, Gerda began the very subtle separation process from her parents, yet not in such a way that she would now have begun to fight with her parents. She just didn't idealize everything that they had done and everything they had represented, and still do represent. She now stopped discussing her problems with them.

HOWEVER, SHE STILL had a hard time with the problem of her envy. She was convinced of the fact that one did not need to feel envy, and that one certainly did not need to envy one's own children. It was only when I pointed out that envy could be used as an impetus for bringing the people she envied into her life in some way that she was better able to own the problem of her envy. As a result, an increasing number of envy-inducing things came to light. Envy was no longer only triggered by her daughter, but also by her sons and her husband. On the whole, it wasn't a destructive sort of envy, but rather a painful feeling that showed her just how often she had subordinated her own desires and needs.

Through her separation strategies with regards to her parents, Gerda became more sensitive to her own children's attempts to separate. Based on her own experience, she could now understood that when a child leaves its parents it has guilt feelings, even if this separation is a natural part of life.

However, if these feelings of guilt are not addressed and articulated as such, then they are repressed. This manifests itself in the fact that parents are attributed the role of scapegoats by their children. The parents are burdened with all the blame: they are blamed for what they have really neglected to do, and blamed for everything that has possibly transpired in an unhappy relationship between primary caregiver and child. The precise content of our father and mother complexes also comes into play. In addition, parents are ascribed the blame for the fact that the world is not perfect and society not the way it should be. These guilt feelings are manifest both in the reproaches that are expressed, as well as in those that are not. Children's express criticism of their parents serves the separation process by trying to make it clear to them that the parents are at odds with the idealization that the children once held. Frequently, the criticism is launched with great vehemence and is still part of an attempt to get the parents to change and conform to an ideal. As such, it generally does not only have to do with the parents: if we didn't have to say goodbye to the idealizations we have of our parents, then neither would we have to say goodbye to the idealizations we have of ourselves. We might also be able to salvage this ideal. Letting go of these idealizations means trusting that they are not viable, and being happy that we don't have to be so perfect after all. In letting go of idealizations, we are free to look at reality as it is. Being realistic is something that is reflected in the way that we act, since in the final analysis, our dreams are not always within reach. Instead of relinquishing idealizations, what often happens is that parents and children try to educate one another about things that need to change. Parents are eager to quickly and thoroughly make up for what they have missed in life so far. Adolescents, on the other hand, want to exact retribution from their parents for what they supposedly—or really—did do and they attack whenever they feel that they have been hard done by. Of course these mutual attempts at education are torpedoed by both sides, and for the most part they have quite a negative impact on the relationship. Nevertheless, everyone rigidly adheres to their own position. And this means that no one lets go. In fact, quite the opposite occurs: parents and children become firmly locked onto one another. If it were possible to relate to the other person, to see them as a human being replete with possibilities and limitations, and less in their role as either parent or child, then it might be possible to see in these attempts at mutual education ways in which pain about the necessary separation could be avoided, and ways in which old conflicts could be resolved.

This dynamic of parents and children trying in vain to change one another was clearly apparent in the separation processes of Gerda's children. All reproaches and attempts by Gerda's children to educate her stopped abruptly when she was finally able to bring herself to say that she was happy that her children were more independent than she herself had ever been. She also said that she felt that she had acted in the right way, even if it had nearly done her in. From this point on, the children were less rebellious, were more willing to engage in conversation at home, and above all spoke about what it had meant to them to have a fearful mother and a much less fearful father.

A NEW PROBLEM arose when Gerda stopped waiting on her children, and began to pursue her own interests. This took both her and her husband away from home more often. Now the children protested. Nothing was the way it had been in the past; there was no relying on their mother anymore. She might not be depressed any longer, might not be critical, not even implicitly, but she wasn't around any more when they needed her: they couldn't depend on her. The children wanted to sabotage this phase in the grieving process of their parents, a phase in which their mother established a new relationship with the self and with the world at large. They wanted to keep their mother as she was. They also sensed the change in their parents' marriage dynamic. Gerda was less fearful than she had been. She had become more independent, self-reliant, and as such, more interesting and exciting to her husband. Added to that was the fact that because Gerda had learned to let go, it was no longer necessary for her husband to frantically retreat. They both suddenly discovered interests that they could share with one another. It was above all Gerda who allowed the desires of her youth to surface again, and her husband was happy to let himself be stimulated by these impulses. Evidently he was also glad to suddenly find himself the center of his wife's attentions again—just as he had been at the beginning of their relationship. She had been first and foremost a mother, something she herself would have admitted. Together with her husband, they were a reliable married couple that functioned well and could balance one another out. For all that, Gerda had hardly been a partner to her husband: that had been her lowest priority.

Gerda's parents were also dissatisfied. They found their daughter, now middle-aged, becoming quite eccentric. By joining forces with their grandchildren, they tried to oblige Gerda to resume her old ways of behaving. Gerda could understand her parents' reaction because she had experienced something similar with regards to her own children. She wanted to explain to them what had transpired, but her parents didn't hear her. Finally she had to accept that she must take these steps without the blessing of her parents, and that this was also an appropriate step for her. In so doing, she thought of herself as "grown up," and responsible. The reproaches from her children gave her more to contend with. She was unsure whether or not some of the children's demands weren't perhaps justified. And she felt the temptation to give in to these demands, to reestablish the old relationships. At the same time, she didn't want to let herself be hindered in her new way of life.

IN THE PROCESS of separating, adolescents use their parents' home as a homebase, so to speak, a place that they can always reach out to. Subsequent to this separation phase comes a phase of reattachment. This reattachment phase is often misunderstood by parents and children alike to mean that everything is now fine and that life can resume again as it was before. Reattachment is, however, quickly followed by a reattachment crisis which leads to the next phase of separation. This process can progress considerably more smoothly if it is mutually understood that the pit-stop at home serves the purpose of giving reassurance that we are loved and accepted, even if we ultimately have to make our own way in life. That means, of course, that the parents (or the mother) has to keep herself available at all times. This is where the adolescents' rebellion against all the new changes comes into play. Adolescents do indeed want everything to change, and yet at the same time, they want everything to stay the same at home. The phase during which parents were totally available has come to an end with the separation, which is just how things should be. Given these changes, it would make sense for adolescents as well as parents to do their grief work.

With Gerda, it became apparent that her separation from the mother-role necessitated grieving work. She became depressed because she had suppressed all feelings of grief. When she did apply herself to the long overdue work of grieving, she succeeded not only in letting go of the children: she found she could let go of them in such a way that she was not left with the feeling of having been robbed. Instead, she lived on in conscious knowledge of the rich life that she had had with her children. Over and again she experienced a slight sadness about the fact that things were no longer as they had been. She could, however, accept these changes without calling into question her value as a mother and a woman. She also accepted her new phase of life. The initial "anxiety work" [14] in connection with menopause had now been achieved. Through the separation process from her children, she had finally learned how to separate from her own parents, but without going overboard. The relationship with her husband had been given a new lease.

# The Difficulties in Finding a New Identity

◆

## The Meaning of Identity

THROUGH THE PROCESS OF GRIEVING, we learn to let go of our communal self and to reconstitute ourselves as individuals. This reorganization of the self as an individual entity is something that we also have to accomplish in the grief work associated with separating from our children. Although our relationship with the children usually continues, a serious grieving process has something to be said for it—the children have been relinquished and have left the family, and the relationship with them is radically different from before. If the separation is really completed—and that means that everyone has gone through a mourning period—then it will also seem easier to regard the children as grown-up people with whom we can enter into new relationships. Depending on how things work out, these mature children may at some point even have to assume a kind of parental role themselves when they come to care for their own aged parents.

IN ORDER TO be able to reconstitute the self from a communal entity to an individual one, we first have to have an awareness of our own individuality. We must have a feeling for our own particular identity and cannot exist as a derivative identity. We speak of a derivative identity when, for example, a woman defines herself exclusively in terms of her relationship with her child or her husband. An autonomous identity is, however, what is necessary for a healthy life.

Our identity is based on the feeling of corporeality and associated with that, the feeling of vitality and the sense of being alive.[15] Rooted in this feeling is the capacity to actively manifest the ego in life and, ultimately, to fulfill our potential. Vitality, ego-activity, and self-realization are all interconnected. Ego-activity is increasingly manifest as self-determination, rather than heteronomy, during the course of a person's development. Throughout our lives, we take a risk being active and, associated with this, we take a risk in expressing who we are. In so doing, we experience our limitations, more or less painfully, and this means that we become conscious of our own ego-complex, often simply called the "self."

The process of living our own identity is also accompanied by a certain self-knowledge: an awareness about the image that we have of ourselves, how this is differentiated from, and conflicts with, the images that other people have and bring to bear on us. A prerequisite for this differentiated ego-complex is that, appropriate to the child's age, the ego-complex differentiates itself from the ego-complexes of the parents. In so doing, the individual becomes increasingly independent and exposes him or herself to new relationships and experiences.

These identity boundaries can be seen as being both preliminary and mutable. Becoming a self means continually redrawing the boundaries between oneself and the rest of the world, between the ego and the unconscious. The experience of having secure boundaries also allows us to dissolve boundaries. We experience this in love and sex, for example, when we feel as though we are merging with another person. A certain loss of ego can be tolerated because we know that we can always reorganize the self within its boundaries again.

Continuity is something else that belongs to the process of living out our own identity. The knowledge that despite all the changes and this process of becoming, we will still stay ourselves. Being conscious of our links to our ancestors and descendants also contributes to the feeling of continuity. We experience continuity above all in our emotional lives; our emotions follow a biological pattern. Even though this pattern barely changes during the course of a lifetime, we can nevertheless change the way we deal with our emotions. We experience emotions physically.

Such physical sensations create the basis of the ego-complex. They are responsible for the fact that we experience ourselves in a continuity and are conscious of our own identity.

Self-interest, concern about how we function and what we achieve, and also the fantasies that we have about ourselves, all belong to the experience of identity. As a result, there is a constant struggle between who we are and who we want to be. Aspects of ourselves that we cannot reconcile with our own self-image become suppressed, become our "shadows."[16]

Autonomy is an important part of the experience of identity. We do not become completely autonomous during the course of our lives, but rather we pass through stages of increasing autonomy. The dependencies remain, and there are also new ones that arise with the passage of time. Yet in the more autonomous aspects of our identities, where we perceive that we are really true to ourselves, dependence is replaced by independence, and the responsibilities associated with independence. As a result, we are not just determined by parental relationships, are no longer programmed by our parents' "tapes," and in general, we are less swayed by the views of people in authority. This means that we also venture to implement our own plans in the world and are responsible for our own endeavors.

A person who is engaged in this developmental process from dependence and restriction to increasing autonomy and the capacity for relationships, can be said to have an independent self. In the Jungian sense this also means that the feeling of identity is rooted in the experience of an underlying guiding principle in life. This guiding principle is manifest in the form of various symbols in our consciousness and directs the construction of the ego-complex and, with it, the so-called individuation process.[17]

THIS DEVELOPMENT OF an autonomous identity is decisively initiated during adolescence by the separation from the parents, and by dissociation from the father- and mother-complexes.

When a girl enters adolescence, the first thing to be activated is the father-complex in its general aspect. Of course this father-complex is manifest in different ways, depending on how the girl personally experienced her father. This means that for the first time, men become interesting to her; life qualities that were associated with the father, are projected in a new, somewhat altered form onto friends. Alternatively, the qualities may be superimposed onto spiritual and intellectual life. Both socialization forms have a certain fascination, and can appear simultaneously. As a rule, however, we have on the one hand girls who find boyfriends very early and live in partner relationships. On the other hand, there are those who choose an intellectual life for themselves, who move in a spiritual world, motivated by inspiration, religion, or politics, and for whom the fascination with the intellect and intelligence plays a big role. Depending on the underlying mother-complex, these girls are more or less asexual during this phase.

In both socialization forms, ties to the father and the father-complex remain intact, even when the two socialization forms are able to coexist. An altercation with the father-complex is not required of the girl, because in identifying with the father-complex the girl can adequately fulfill the social role demanded of her: Either she has a boyfriend and soon becomes a housewife and mother—and she does not oppose her husband by exerting her own will—or she enters the intellectual world, generally associated with the father role, and she proves herself there. There is, of course, no objection to be made against either choice of role if it is the result of a girl's own decision and does not just reflect an arrested stage of development. The latter can result in the fact that the girl never seeks an autonomous identity. Instead, she assumes a prescribed identity.

Women whose ego-complex is identified with the father-complex invariably know just how to conduct themselves in the world, how to work hard, and so on. Yet for all this, it is surprising that when these women experience emotional breakdowns—for example, a separation or the children leaving home—they feel empty, destroyed, and cannot fathom their own behavior. Up until this point, they had got along very well in life and had always been so rational! If a woman has not tackled the issue of her father- and mother-complexes and has simply transferred the father-complex to her male partner, then the woman can remain stuck for a long time in the role of a daughter. As such, she is not her husband's partner. Instead, she is secretly the daughter of her husband. This is also a form of the derivative identity. The derivative identity is frequently seen as being desirable and as a result, it is not problematized by society. The demands of the role may conflict with the chosen identity of the woman, at least she is able to fulfill the expected role without having to search for an identity. She feels she is a "real woman" and because she is fulfilling her role, is never forced to ask herself what her role actually is. That she has no identity of her own does not seem to occur to her.

## From a Derivative Identity to an Autonomous Identity

A STUDY BY Bernardoni and Werder[18] shows that eight out of ten successful women who occupy leading positions in their professions had fathers who were academics and who ensured that their daughters became independent and self-reliant. In this study, the father was described as the role model for these women. He was generally depicted as dynamic, active, intelligent, ambitious, and liberal. That these women described their fathers in such positive terms ought not necessarily be attributed to idealization. It is conceivable that the fathers described in the study really were as attractive as they were made out to be. If this is true, then by contrast the role of the mother would have been very unappealing to these women. The mothers were rejected because the successful women could not accept the passivity and blandness of their submissive mothers. The identification with the father and the suppression of the mother role may have already led to identity problems during adolescence. In instances where the adolescents encountered problems, the problems were compensated for by overachieving. Of the women dealt with in this study, one could say that they generally had positive father-complexes. Most of the women were married and the researchers observed laconically that the marriages were under even greater stress than most marriages. At least outwardly, the women would clearly defer to their husbands.

I have cited this study because, in my view, it illustrates an important contemporary socialization form, namely identification with the father role—obviously the more attractive option. Identifying with the father role means, however, that the ego-complex comes to be identified with the father-complex. The mother-complex and also the relationship with the mother are split off and assume a background role. The cause of this identification with the father-complex has to do with both the attractiveness of the father role and the fact that the daughter never comes into conflict with the mother role. If this conflict does not take place during adolescence, then it generally occurs during middle age. Against this background, women frequently find themselves having severe identity crises when they are forced to separate from their children, when they go through menopause, and with separation in general.

THE CONFLICT WITH the female identity has to take place during adolescence. If it does not, then rather than having an autonomous identity, the woman is saddled with a derivative one, an identity that is prescribed by the outside world, perhaps by the men in her life, or by collective expectations of what her role should be. What is lacking is an autonomous identity, an identity that takes into account the special inner world of the woman in question. Finding such an autonomous identity is not easy. When women look for female role models that might be appropriate for them, it often turns out that the role models comprise male images, specifically images that men have made of women. In fact, a lot of conscious effort is demanded of women, if women are to construct for themselves an identity that is not a derivative one. They must consciously work to describe their feelings of identity, to search for images that correspond to their own inner constitutions, images that do not simply mirror random external expectations. Naturally, these women's images will ultimately be a composite between inner and outer worlds, a mixture of old images drawn from the expectations of the primary caregivers and from the image that is linked to one's inner life.

The necessity of finding one's own identity seems to

me to be an extraordinarily significant starting point for the emancipation of women. It might not be a spectacular starting point and might be arduous to carry out, but it is nevertheless of great importance. The position of women will not be fundamentally improved as long as women let their own identities be withheld from them.

In order to find their own identities, women have to take their own mothers to task. Should this conflict not take place during adolescence, then the problems associated with the mother are generally carried over to the partner and compound the difficulties of the partnership.

## *The Conflict with the Mother*

EVEN WHEN THE daughter's conflict with her mother takes place during adolescence, the conflict still begins with the setting up of boundaries. At first the conflict is about the actual mother and the role that she has chosen for her life: the mother embodies a model that is initially contrary to the identity that is unconsciously chosen by the daughter. In the daughter's choice of a counter-identity, the mother's shadow, her unaccepted and unloved sides, play a role. Daughters whose mothers pursue a rather ascetic way of life may, for example, cultivate an extravagant lifestyle in early adolescence. In so doing, they indirectly show their mothers everything that their mothers have missed in life. This, incidentally, may provoke the mothers into rethinking their entire lifestyle. However, mothers usually react with shock and fear, more shock and fear than is in fact warranted. Parents need not really worry since a child is influenced by its mother throughout its childhood and youth and the image of the mother is deeply imprinted on its personality. Sooner or later the image of the mother will exert its influence. Unfortunately, this means that there is far less revolutionary change in the development of the human race than one would hope. What ensues—postadolescence—is frequently not even a real compromise between the ideals that the parents have passed on through their style of child-rearing, and the converse of these ideals. Instead, one generally finds that people grow up and adopt a lifestyle that is clearly determined by the values of their family of origin.

Initially, however, the shadow is used as a means of establishing boundaries. During this phase, girls tell themselves that they will do everything differently from their mothers. This pronouncement does not necessarily signify a bad relationship with the mother. It is primarily an expression of the search for an identity. This search begins with the setting up of boundaries against the mother.

In actual fact, at this stage the girl does not have any real position of her own. She is just "against everything." Taking a stand against everything conveys the erroneous impression that one has a position of one's own, a conviction that certainly helps the process along, provided the search for an independent identity does not stop here. In this search for self-understanding and a lifestyle that is contrary to that of the mother, the girl launches into a search for female role models. She might try out different lifestyles—either concretely or in her imagination—including fantasized lifestyles which are oriented towards women and which can serve as role models. Given that girls adopt role models as a natural part of their development, it seems to me that the type of projections made about women are of the utmost importance. Role models might be drawn from contemporary living women or from women's biographies which are to be found in ever increasing numbers. Whatever the source, the role model might have little in common with the adolescent's actual living situation. The posture adopted by the girl is the first expression of the image of women that she has appropriated in her own unconscious. To the extent that it is not just a repressed life-plan, the posture that she assumes will emerge most easily in the proximity of a really autonomous image of women, an autonomous image of the self, that will naturally change and metamorphose over time.

It is not only role models that play an important part in this differentiation phase, which is actually a phase of finding oneself. Also important are relationships with other women; that is, assuming that the imprint of the mother-complex permits such a thing. Should a woman be stamped by a very negative mother-complex, then women—particularly motherly ones—will only be a source of disappointment to her. In this case, the option of having important relationships with other women will probably not be available. Generally speaking, having relationships with other women enables one to become conscious of oneself as a woman. Women then see themselves not only with their own eyes, but also through the eyes of another woman. They mirror one another, take themselves seriously, accept themselves. The relationship to other women also conveys an experiential quality. By this I mean that it can best be described by the term "anima-quality": an atmosphere of mutual connectedness and, by extension, a spiritual "expansiveness"; a way of not having to protect oneself; a way of being erotically appealing that does not demand immediate action; a fascination with feminine possibilities, and tenderness that can simply be tried out.[19] In relating to other women, unconscious female images are conjured up and come to be associated with the respective emotions that belong to the different female images. These feelings have a lot to do with connectedness—tender solidarity, fierce bonds—and open up different dimensions of womanhood. Originally, Jung considered "anima" to be the feminine aspect in a man's soul. A woman, on the other hand, had an "animus." However, women's need for "anima" seems to be very great, and it is vital for breaking out of the mother-complex. The exchange of experiences with girlfriends and the emotional interaction between them are very important in the development of a girl's own self-image. Such relationships can only occur if they are not relegated to a subordinate position because the relationship with a boyfriend is deemed more important by family or society. Exchanges between women promote the development of relationship structures that allow a woman to be herself, rather than encourage her to give herself up. Women are afforded the space to experience and cultivate differentiated feelings within the relationship.

A new life-plan crystallizes out of the experience of relating to other women. This, in turn, permits the daughter to reapproach the mother. Generally, a conflict with the mother is now handled in an empathetic manner, rather than aggressively as before. The mother can now be seen as an independent personality, she can be understood in the context of her own process of coming-into-being. This phase of reapproaching the mother also brings with it the awareness of the peculiarities that we share with our mothers. We may even find that we have the very same annoying qualities, and that at best we can try to learn to deal with them differently. Nevertheless, we realize that in spite of the similarities, we are indeed quite different. This reapproachment might be manifest in conversations, in which it becomes clear to the daughter why the mother chose the course of life that she did. These conversations might also contribute to the mother's understanding of her daughter's life-plan. On the other hand, we could be forced to accept, albeit reluctantly, that we have chosen a course of life that our mother skeptically opposes, that she might not be able to accept it because of her own history. The reapproachment crisis comes about because of a sense of disappointment that something has passed: the former relationship between mother and child (when the mother and daughter were perhaps the best of friends) can never be recreated. The crisis can also be manifest as a thwarted hope that mother and daughter might finally be able to achieve something that they have fantasized about, but which has hitherto eluded them— the development of a close relationship. They have to reconcile themselves to the fact that the best thing that can be achieved is a good, trusting relationship between mother and daughter, a relationship between women who know one another well, who value one another, and accept that there are different ideas of what it means to be a woman.

## Daughters Separating
## from Their Mothers

DAUGHTERS' SEPARATION from their mothers takes place in a complex and difficult environment. It is further complicated by the respective personal problems between mother and daughter.

MOTHERS WITH LITTLE SELF-AWARENESS – In her book, *When Mothers Work*,[20] Scarr reports that mothers who work and enjoy what they do have daughters who grow up having more self-awareness. These daughters are also less willing to place themselves in dependent positions, even when they are thoroughly ensconced in the father's world. This means that self-aware mothers have daughters who are themselves more self-aware. But the converse is also true: daughters of mothers who draw their self-worth from the acceptance of family members in turn have difficulty establishing their value as women. Mothers have all the more difficulty because the acceptance accorded them does not generally increase over time; it diminishes. The mother is criticized because the daughter has to separate from her, and out of habit she very quickly gets used to the tenderest comforting.

However, it is not just a question of the woman, particularly the housewife and mother, being accepted by family members. At the time of her separation from the children, acceptance is probably at an all-time low. It has far more to do with the fact that on top of everything else, women are still undervalued in our culture. The subtle put-down of women can be distinguished from obvious depreciation strategies when, for example, a teenage boy concurs with his father that well, "it's only mum" who is against it, and the father does not correct his son. Subtle depreciation strategies are, for example, manifest in the fact that men's arguments are automatically given more weight than women's; that women may well perform all manner of tasks, but not have any say when decisions are made; that in any case it is men rather than women who do the talking, thereby drawing attention to themselves; women are less easily heard. Subtle depreciation strategies are also manifest in pitying glances and offers of help that are not necessary. Ultimately, women suffer from this learned helplessness.[21]

And this surreptitiously, terribly undervalued gender is what one is supposed to belong to as a girl. It is not easy. It does become easier, though, if one's own mother and the men in the family are aware of the insidious depreciating remarks and, as a result, try to make changes. It helps, in other words, if vigilance about the prevailing image of women is made tangible.

THE "DEVOURING MOTHER"—A MISLEADING EXPRESSION – The concept of the "devouring mother" occurs frequently in psychology. The expression means different things: on the one hand, it implies mothers who do not want to let go of their children, who will not relinquish them so that they can pursue their own lives; on the other hand, it also denotes those women and men who are inhibited by their mother-complexes, who, for example, are prevented from becoming autonomous.

As Christa Rohde-Dachser also suggests,[22] the expression "devouring mother" is shaped by a fear of the mother and the fear of the feminine. Devouring: the expression clearly suggests that the feminine is dangerous, and unconsciously this supposed element of danger becomes an additional reason for depreciating the feminine. In the field of depth psychology, itself stamped by male psychology, the expression "devouring mother" is associated with the following, for instance: the Great Mother, the archetypal mother, the principle of the motherly in life, represented by the different mother goddesses. She is also designated by the term "devouring mother" when she is represented as the goddess of death, who having given her life in such rich abundance, finally takes life back into the womb of the earth. Birth and death are archetypically associated with the feminine principle. Birth and death—although death perhaps not exclusively so—have almost always been symbolized by goddesses. Women do indeed bear children into a life that knows suffering, pain, and death. It is, however, foolish to project this life principle onto concrete women, ultimately to burden them with the responsibility for the existence of suffering, pain, and death. Yet this is just what happens when concepts like the "devouring mother" are used thoughtlessly and then naturally projected onto concrete women. By projecting the concept onto real women, they become the "devouring mothers," even when it is simply a case of them having some difficulty letting go of their children. As I have already stated, the expression refers to the fear of the maternal. The foundations for this fear of the maternal are manifold. In the life of a human being, there operates a more or less well-founded fear of not becoming autonomous. There is the fear that we might regress, get bogged down in life and, for example, search out a good mother who enables us to spend our entire life as the spoiled son. It is also possible that the mother-complex, which has been activated by love, can lead to a great enslavement to a woman. Be that as it may, there is still no need to speak of "devouring mothers" in a very generalized way.

Considerably less mention is made of mothers who sacrifice their lives in the service of other people. Of the many different ways of seeing the feminine and the maternal, the "feminine as dangerous" is the viewpoint that prevails. This perspective is unduly transferred onto the individual woman, who is simultaneously idealized. She is put on a pedestal because she sacrifices her life, but at the same time, she is seen as bringing death, and has to be devalued to counter the idealization. Yet she really is "only" a human being, and not a goddess. This is one aspect of the irritating situation in which mothers find themselves today, and something that tempers the contradictory way in which the mother role is seen.

For the woman and for the girl, this projection means the realization that there is something very dangerous, or at least something ambivalent, associated with being a woman, that there is perhaps even something monstrous about her womanhood, something that she can neither know nor fathom.

In recent times, there has been a lot of consciousness-raising work done on issues associated with the perception of women: The different goddesses (not just the mother goddesses and certainly not only the devouring ones), but also the love goddesses, the goddesses of wisdom, the wise women[23] and so on, are all now being examined and described by women. It is a large-scale attempt undertaken by many women to make women in general, conscious and appreciative of the archetypical roots of their existence.

The project offers images of womanhood which having been transformed by personal fantasy, can then become images for the self. In adopting these images, it seems to me that it is crucially important that we take the liberty and the trouble to transform these archetypal images using our own fantasies. We need to reconstitute them according to our own individuation, so that they too do not just become self-images that are imposed on us by the outside world.

All these models of femininity also correspond to typical types of relationships and to certain forms of sexuality. But the following is true as well: the identification with an idealized, archetypal image does not, in and of itself, provide us with an image of ourselves, does not generate an autonomous identity. It is only through reworking, through our conflict with these archetypal images, that our own independent self-image can develop. In conjunction with the contemporary consciousness-raising about archetypal forms of women, women's autobiographies are also partially uncovering the yet to be emphasized desire for female role models.

THE SHAM EXISTENCE AND THE DELEGATION OF LIFE'S POSSIBILITIES – The process of mother-daughter separation is further complicated by the fact that mothers are not always truthful about their lives. One hears again and again about mothers who convey the idea to their adolescent daughters that a life with a husband and child is the only thing worth striving for. Later, it transpires that these mothers were actually unhappy with their lot in life. Nevertheless, they recommended the very same thing to their daughters. As a result, middle-aged women often criticize their mothers for having portrayed unrealizable lifestyles as attractive. They take issue with the fairy tales about handsome princes that they were told about by their mothers.

Daughters also address the problem of delegating. Mothers who have not lived their own lives often have the tendency to project their own unheeded desires and potential onto their daughters. The daughters are then supposed to bring into fruition whatever has been denied the mothers. Thus, the unfulfilled possibilities in life are delegated to the subsequent generation. The straight-forward delegation, something that sons obviously have to contend with as well, is relatively simple to deal with. Provided that children are aware of the expectations and can bring themselves to make boundaries, they can generally circumvent their parents' expectations. The situation becomes problematic, however, when mothers voice contradictory expectations. They may, for example, convey to their daughters the indisputable life dictum that, as a woman, one can only be independent by earning one's own living. In expressing this conviction, they really mean, "Become a professional woman!" As a subtext, however, the mothers often make observations that would suggest that they think that without children and a family one is not in fact a real woman. The dynamic is even more problematic when the message goes something like this, "Whatever you do, just don't live the kind of a life I have, but by the same token, don't make any more of your life than I have made of mine."

In making this sort of delegation, mothers who have made too little out of their lives leave a difficult legacy of guilt for their daughters. The daughters' difficulties are compounded by their mothers' ambivalent reactions to their chosen lifestyles. As we all know, it is not possible for women who have denied themselves a great deal in life to look on with equanimity and without envy as the younger generation experiments in the work sphere, or as it tries out relationships and sexuality.

IN ADDITION TO these general problems, which have yet to be adequately articulated and overcome in the separation between mother and child, there is also a whole array of personal problems which mother and child have with one another, and which arise out of their mutually shared life story. Aside from this, there are quite often problems that have remained unsolved and unconscious in one's own mother-daughter relationship which get repeated by the subsequent generation.

Yet in spite of all these difficulties, the work of separating has to be accomplished if the daughter is to actually come to have her own female identity. Mother and daughter must separate if the daughter is to find a self that is her own autonomous self, one that affords her the capacity for increasing self-realization during the course of her life, and that enables her to recapture herself in the wake of separation, parting, and loss. Founded upon an ever-increasingly autonomous self, she does not always have to conform to other people's desires just so that she can have her own self-worth confirmed. She knows from within the measure of her own worth. Her self-worth is made tangible by virtue of the fact that she is who she is, she accepts herself, and she takes herself seriously. Grounded in her own self, she can build balanced relationships with other people and also with the patriarchal world, if that should be the course she sets herself.[24]

# Separation Work When Grieving Seems Impossible

♦

ANNA, FIFTY-TWO, FEELS THAT HER LIFE is empty and barren, she sleeps badly, awakens early, then worries about her children, but is not capable of precisely articulating just what these worries are. "Things might not go well for them in life, they might give up." If they go on a trip, she doesn't have "a single peaceful moment" until they are home, safe and sound. Lately, her husband has also been very "stressed out." He has a job with a lot of responsibility and feels threatened by younger co-workers who constantly want to change things. According to Anna, "He's not doing so well either," so she has to do everything she can to make sure that there is an atmosphere at home that allows him to relax. In other words, she does not tell him anything of her own troubles.

"Sometimes he also says, 'You have it good now that

there's not that much work, life's got to be pretty ok.'
Then I believe him again. But actually it's not true, I'm
not doing that well. I don't sleep, I can't get going in the
mornings; that much is obvious. I don't feel good, I have
the feeling that I have a lot of work to do, that I can't get
it all done; my husband says that of course I can. Everything is so banal, and I can't change anything. And then on
top of everything else, I've developed this strange backpain.
The doctor can't find anything physically wrong, but
sometimes I think, it's not only my back, absolutely everything hurts...."

Anna is indeed constantly busy; that is, apart from
the hours she spends lying in bed, worrying about something or other. Yet she is not fulfilled, she is even bored.
She says she really does want to do all the things that will
make her husband's life easier for him, but after protracted
conversations, it turns out that she simply regards it as
being her duty; it's all for nought. She has the feeling that
her husband takes for granted everything she does for
him. She doesn't get any praise; on the contrary, she hears
repeated remarks about how she is getting older, and that
she doesn't have the same get-up-and-go that she used to.

The fact that Anna's gloomy thoughts in the early
morning hours revolve around her children could signify
that she has a problem with her children, possibly a problem with separation, and that this could be at the root of
her quite marked depressive malaise. In addition, she and
her husband seem to have difficulty with the fact that

they are becoming older, yet have not actually consciously looked these difficulties in the eye.

When asked about the difficulties of separation, at first Anna spares herself through a show of bravery by saying, "That's something that all parents have to go through." She says that at least she has had the good fortune that all of her children have turned out well, although she does add that "unfortunately" they have gotten very little care and help "in return" from their children. This is "unfortunately" just the way things go today. According to Anna, this could hardly be the reason for her general bad humor. It's true that she misses the children very much, but one has to get over all that.

She wonders whether her worries about her husband might not be the reason behind her insomnia. And whether perhaps these worries might not be a justified source of concern? Perhaps her husband is in extreme danger, he might well die soon, he might be deathly ill? I corroborated her fear that we really never know when a person with whom we are involved is going to die. I asked her whether she feels the need to particularly spoil him, maybe to give him something that she has not given him up until now. No, she wouldn't have any of that. Instead, she said that she had the irrepressible feeling that her husband should finally, once and for all, do something for her. The aggression she felt towards her husband was tangible when she spoke about him. It was manifest as the fear of death, but was in actual fact an averted death-wish. From her line of argumentation one could also surmise that she is afraid of not getting what is rightfully hers in life.

It is typical of people with an distinctly depressive constitution that they always try to suit other people, who then get used to such treatment. As a result, depressive people are often overlooked when it comes to them getting what they would like to have in life. It is a great help if people with a depressive make-up can learn to precisely formulate what it is that they would like from their fellow human beings and, in so doing, also risk being rejected or misunderstood. Anna, however, was not yet ready for such a step. Nothing concrete came to mind when she was asked what her husband could either do for her or should do differently. Nevertheless, it was obvious that there was a source of dissatisfaction in the present relationship, even though it was not clear initially whether Anna was not perhaps projecting onto her husband the rage she felt about her grown children, who by her own account didn't give anything back.

I tried to initiate grief work with her, by asking her to recount the various qualities her children—she had two girls and a boy—had brought to life in her. For hours she told me stories about her children, what they had been like, what they had gotten up to, but nothing about what the children had awakened in her. It became increasingly clear that she felt that she had had the most wonderful children in the world and that they were now in relationships with people who had spoiled them. As a result, one could no longer expect anything from them. They were in effect lost to her. By way of example, she explained that her son would definitely want to come and visit her more often—he visited her about twice a week, and three times since she had been feeling poorly—but his girlfriend had something against it. Anna has never spoken about this with him in order to check out her assumption, but she is convinced that things are the way she thinks they are.

In the face of these changed life circumstances, Anna is seized by feelings of aggression which are directed at other people who exist outside of the family system. As a consequence, they become enemies whom she finds increasingly threatening. This only increases her fear even more. That she feels bad in the current situation becomes increasingly apparent the longer she talks about her family. Even if one takes into consideration the fact that her characterizations are grossly idealized—which in and of itself shows the extent to which she has had to ward off the anger that she thought she ought not feel—one is nevertheless left with the impression that her life as a housewife, spent caring for her children, had completely fulfilled her. She and her husband both seemed to have been enthusiastic parents and the grown children were, in their own way, thankful for this. They invited their parents to their parties, for example; one daughter had a standing engagement with her mother to take a long walk every two weeks. From an outsider's point-of-view, the children gave their parents a great deal in return. Yet Anna could not see things like this. Everything was supposed to be the way it used to be; anything else was just not good enough.

Anna was also upset that she was having such difficulties. She did in fact concede that her health in the last few years was not what it had been, namely robust, cheerful, more easy-going, but that probably had something to do with menopause. Now she had "gone through all that," but she was worse off than ever before.

Anna's story is a very straightforward case history and, as it seems to me, one that is quite typical for women. She was the second oldest daughter, the second daughter in a family of six children; after Anna there followed a series of exclusively male siblings. Her father was "a strong person," he determined what went down at home, a place where order prevailed. Her mother, on the other hand, was quiet. In later life, she sufferingly sacrificed herself for the well-being of the family and died at the age of sixty-four. The mother was only taken seriously by the family when she was not there, or when she was ill. Then it became clear to the family what an enormous workload she had.

In identifying with their mother, the girls learned "to be there for the men." Anna related this with pride. She went on in a similar vein about how all three were very handy about the house and how much they had liked to do this sort of work. Now, in hindsight, she said that she certainly thinks often about her mother and asks herself whether she might not in fact have also sometimes had other desires and whether she hadn't been very depressed as well. But at the time, her father had let it be known that everyone in the family was supposed to be happy, so everyone just was happy. Anna did not learn any particular skills. She went to the French-speaking part of Switzerland and worked there in a household. In so doing, she got to know her husband, who was living in a pension at the time, while he went to school there. "He knew his way around life almost as well as my father, and I liked him a whole lot. He was cheerful and also a bit more high-spirited than my father." Anna's parents insisted, however, that they might only marry when they were nineteen-years-old; she was seventeen when she first got to know her husband. In the meantime, her husband learned English in England, she went back to her parents, helped her mother with all the housework, and concerned herself with her dowry.

After they were married, Anna and her husband both moved to a neighboring town. They had their first apartment of their own—and she found it all just wonderful. Soon thereafter, she became pregnant—and she was happy about that. Between the births of the three children there were long stretches of time, which was not something that she had actually planned on. Anna had increasing difficulty becoming pregnant. As a result, the pleasure was all the greater when eight years after the birth of her second daughter, she became pregnant again at the age of thirty-two. After that her interest in her own sex life diminished sharply. She was now with all her heart and soul a mother to these children, and her husband seemed to be a similarly enthusiastic parent.

Only after a long time in therapy did she mention that she had had repeated miscarriages, most shortly after the beginning of the pregnancy, roughly in the second month. She could not recall exactly how many miscarriages she had had, but she also didn't think it that important, because of course "it" came beforehand. Nevertheless, it became clear during the course of the therapeutic conversation that she had had a hard time coping with these miscarriages, that she had now and again asked herself whether she was in fact a real woman. Her husband had always reassured her that she was a wonderful woman, and then her apprehension was dispelled again.

IN THIS LIFE STORY, one can see that a concrete transferal has taken place, from the father to the husband. Anna was, so to speak, given straight from the hands of the father into the hands of the husband, whom she was nonetheless very found of. Even though her mother was a relatively unimposing, albeit very helpful, figure in her family of origin, Anna did identify with her mother. Anna followed her mother's example and did everything just as her mother had done before her. "My mother was a competent woman, I have actually learned everything from her, and I hope that I run my household as well as she did."

In Anna's case, she engaged neither in a conflict with

her father nor her mother, neither with the father-complex nor with the mother-complex. On the one hand, Anna lived in unconscious identification with her mother, and on the other hand, with the role of mother and housewife. As such, she could develop an identity that was just barely autonomous. However, in her current circumstances, she finds that life is compelling her to acquire a new identity, perhaps for the first time an identity that is not a derivative one. She has to separate from the role identity that has hitherto been her own, and must reconstitute herself as an individual entity. Yet she has no individual self, at least not for the moment. Anna has always been led to believe that it is important to be there for other people, to care for others, and to fulfill other people's desires. As a result, she could never comprehend why women her age always had "identity problems," why they were so dissatisfied with the woman's lot. She attributed the anxiety and dissatisfaction of her peers to the fact that they must just have had bad parents, wayward children, and therefore were not fully occupied. To be sure, Anna is very concerned that both of her daughters are not married, that they speak very poorly about marriage. She is, in other words, concerned that they no longer identify with her and her understanding of gender roles. Instead, they are clearly in opposition. They repeatedly ask their mother whether she is satisfied with her life. Her daughters also work, something that they do with pleasure and great conviction, and both have positions with a lot of responsibility.

"They are just more influenced by their father. They are a little alien to me."

It is clear that Anna's depressive ill-humor has something to do with the necessity of separating, not just from her children, but also from the role as mother. Nevertheless, at least initially it was impossible for Anna to go ahead with the grief work, because she had no real self in reserve. There was no self for her to withdraw into, a haven where she could have redrafted herself and emerged anew into life. She would have been happy if I could have given her some advice about what to do and about what would happen to her in the future.

JUNGIAN THERAPY traces a client's impulses towards self-realization, impulses that stem from the psyche and which are manifest in the form of symbols in dreams, imaginings, and the like. If these impulses are heeded, processed, and integrated, they can lead to a persevering approximation of the self. It takes slow and painstaking work (which also carefully considers what is happening between the analyst and client) in order to construct an identity that is no longer a derivative one. Obviously this process generates huge conflicts between external and internal expectations. In Anna's case, the expectations of her husband and son (and above all the perceived external demands) were pitted against her own internal demands for autonomy.

Anna was, for example, convinced that she still had to take care of her husband, even though it was never really clear what that actually meant. In stark contrast to this conviction was a dream she had, in which she lovingly embraced her husband while he gasped for air and chastized her for not leaving him any breathing room.

In the imaginative processing of this dream sequence, Anna gave herself over to the dream images. She allowed the images to metamorphose and then spoke about the process. She came to see that she really was crushing her husband out of "sheer love." Afterwards she asked herself whether smothering her husband actually constituted love, whether that couldn't instead be an expression of hatred. We took this hatred to mean that she allowed too little separation between her husband and herself. Aggression in a relationship often serves the function of creating little separations within the relationship, which in turn allow us to cultivate our individual selves rather than the self that is part of a relationship. In other words, the expression of hatred means that we have difficulty separating, often that we have gone too long without taking some space for ourselves.

ANNA ALSO DREAMT about women her own age and older who lived in Paris and spoke elegant French. These dreams released a great longing in her. She wished that she could move through Paris with the self-assurance of the women in her dreams. In having these dreams, it was not just a matter of Anna longing to speak elegant French—she had of course learned French during her adolescence, even if she had forgotten most of it in the meantime—it also had something to do with erotic fantasies: who knew what a single, older woman, who no longer had to worry about getting pregnant, could experience in Paris? In contrast to Anna, her daughter had an exciting erotic life. Without her daughter ever actually having told her anything specific, the very idea of her daughter's exciting sex life stimulated Anna's fantasies even more and evoked images of womanhood that both fascinated and repulsed her.

These were all images that showed Anna new possibilities opening up for the future. Yet the images were juxtaposed against images in which she was confronted by various authoritarian figures, especially older men who reproached her or restrained her with brute force, as once happened when she dreamt she was trying to board a train for Paris.

Such dreams corresponded to the prevailing feeling that it would be ridiculous at her age to want to change anything, that it would be better to just leave everything as it had been.

Such resignation resulted in the fact that she became more depressed again. At the same time, she found she did not want to resist the transformation process that had been initiated, that it would be better to endure the fear associated with it. The relationship with her husband had in the meantime changed considerably. She could now articulate her desires, and he was rather astonished to find that she did have desires, including sexual ones. He good-naturedly went along with her wishes and found that their relationship was the better for it. As she began to learn to introduce her own wishes into the relationship, Anna was plagued by a great fear: what would happen if her husband would not comply with her wishes, what if he were to reject her, if he were even to leave her? That she was, in fact, much closer to leaving him than he was to leaving her was something that she only came to realize much later. It did not dawn on her until she could admit that her idealization of her husband was the last obstacle to acknowledging that the whole relationship was completely dissatisfying.

In this context I can obviously only depict a few aspects of the protracted therapeutic process. After roughly two years, Anna dreamt repeatedly that she poured a bucket of dirty washwater over the head of a young man, whom she did not recognize. She locked him in his car and, grinning maliciously, threw the car keys into the sea, and once she even shot him.

First of all, we established that these dreams were comprised of layers of meaning. That is to say, we regarded the young man as being one of her personality traits, one that in many ways hindered her from becoming active in life. She fantasized that the young man was aggressive, a bad man, a revolutionary, for example, who would upset the old order of things. We understood that this revolutionary, who was all the while quite active within her personality, had grown up and was now causing her great fear. She was fundamentally afraid of her own aggressive sides, something she was becoming increasingly aware of, repressing less, and finding less easy to project onto other people.

In passing, she mentioned that the young man in her dream wore the same tennis shoes as her son. These tennis shoes were a source of conflict between mother and son: Anna was of the opinion that grown men did not wear tennis shoes. Her son, on the other hand, thought that his mother was no longer in a position to dictate what sort of shoes a grown man should wear. As a result of her realization that the young man was wearing tennis shoes like her son, Anna was able to access the enormous rage she felt towards him. She was angry that he had moved out of home at such a young age and lived with his girlfriend. She was angry about many qualities that he possessed that fundamentally displeased her, and which she had never really addressed before.

An enormous anger also emerged in her relationship with me. It was a strange, impersonal rage. I was suddenly and almost exclusively seen as being the representative of a generation of women who had "simply" pursued a profession, who had earned their own money, were independent, but who naturally couldn't boil an egg and despised housewives. I repeatedly tried to emphasize the fact that I could well understand her anger. There were different paths that women could choose; she could see that just by looking at her daughters. Of course it would

fill one with rage to be confronted by the very embodi-
ment of a course of life that one would have liked to have
embarked upon oneself if only things had gone differently. However, I also told her that I did not entertain any
ill feelings towards women who were housewives and
mothers; and at certain times in one's life, the untraveled
road always seems the more attractive one. On top of all
this, she transferred the rage she felt towards her daughter onto me.

In experiencing this anger, we found ourselves in the
middle of the separation process from her all but grown
children. Suddenly, she realized that the anger she felt had
less to do with the tennis shoes than with the fact her son
had, so to speak, light-footedly slipped out of her care
and control. Now, all at once, she could admit her great
sadness about the fact the old days could never be recap-
tured, that a phase of life was finally over. For the first
time, she could really grieve. She finally understood that
children awaken something in us that we do not have to
lose, provided we do not give it up for lost when the children leave home. She subsequently included her husband
in her memory work. He, in turn, realized he could get
along with his children in a much more relaxed fashion,
once he became conscious of the substance of his relationship with them. He, too, could now admit that a phase
of life was at an end and that he and his wife had to
slowly prepare for old age. Separating from the children
is not only difficult for mothers, it is also hard on fathers.

THIS CASE HISTORY shows that grief work can only be undertaken if a person possesses an individual self to which he or she can retreat and regroup. Women with a derivative identity—and that generally means those who still have a role identity that society deems desirable—often have a depressive constitution. They live their lives for other people and, above all, expect acknowledgement and appreciation from others. They see themselves almost exclusively in the mirror of other people and do not perceive that this sometimes functions as a "distorting mirror." They have difficulties overcoming grief, particularly the grief process associated with separating from their children, because it is so closely associated with a lived identity problem: the mother role has lost its substance and its purpose.

In terms of the therapeutic process, it is not that easy to initiate the grieving process in people who lack a sufficiently independent identity. Before grieving can take place, work has to be done on developing an independent identity. Only then can the actual separation take place.

# Problems in Separating
# from Working Mothers

♦

ALL THE AFOREMENTIONED EXAMPLES might lead one to think that it is only housewives and mothers who have problems in separating from their children. Housewives and mothers probably do have greater difficulty, since their lives have undergone a more radical change than have the lives of working women. The departure of the children means that these women's main sphere of activity has been affected, and it is quite likely that they have no other sphere of life that is equally significant, or almost as significant. Perhaps she has to care for her aging parents as well, a task that involves the expenditure of great physical and emotional resources. This would leave little space or energy to construct a self-chosen sphere of activity, one that is important for her own life, and which could significantly contribute to a sense of fulfillment during the remainder of her life.

Yet separation from the children is not just painful because a phase of life has come to an end and because a central focus of life is no longer sustained. Nor is the separation just painful because one is probably at an age when one starts to go through menopause and asks oneself questions about one's own femininity. By the time one goes through menopause, one can no longer define oneself based solely on one's biological attributes, neither can one draw one's self-worth from the fact that one is sexually attractive and fertile. The pain of separation is compounded because one loses concrete possibilities for fostering relationships with one's children in the microcontext of everyday-life, something that was just taken for granted when they lived at home. Conflict, stimulation, annoyance, tenderness, the dynamic energy of young people are all absent. One can look at it any way one likes, one still loses something that was generally very important, and the freedom that one gained is not an adequate substitute for what has been lost. This is also true for women who work, those who were not exclusively devoted to the well-being of their children and partner. The loss cannot just be denied out of existence. Despite other responsibilities and interests, the loss weighs heavily. Unlike housewives and mothers, however, women who work are similar to men in their capacity to repress the loss. They are able to throw themselves into their work and at least initially often say that they enjoy the diminishing responsibilities on the homefront. Yet, the separation process will also come to have an effect on them. The question of an independent, non-derivative identity, the question of whether one is capable of allowing one's identity to be transformed, and whether one can hear life's call for change are all more important to the process of experiencing and overcoming grief than the issue of whether or not women work.

ANGELA HAS her own boutique that she is very proud of. Ever since she has been married, she has always worked part-time in the boutique and she finally took it over when her youngest child, a daughter, was fourteen. At the time she started therapy, her daughter was twenty-two and had already lived away from home for some years. Angela, now forty-five, could not understand herself. Lately, she had felt so unbalanced, so dissatisfied with life. Suddenly she was no longer satisfied by the relationship with her husband, although in her view, they had both "pulled through" pretty well. Until recently, Angela thought that they actually got along very well together, perhaps not so much as lovers, but as good companions. And that seemed a more attractive prospect any day than having an "ardent lover, whom one could never depend on." She also wondered whether perhaps the impending menopause was casting its pall over her. But since she felt no physical effects of menopause, she dismissed this suspicion.

During therapy she talked about her life, a bout hard times and fulfilling times. Hardly anything was idealized, and also very little was dramatized as overly gloomy. From these stories, I got the impression that Angela was a practical woman, who was basically content with herself, who withstood the conflicts in her marriage and with her parents without feeling resentful. She also seemed to be a woman who did not expect the impossible of herself and thus could also enjoy what she had achieved. It became very clear that she "could not have lived" without working outside of the home. Of course she took great pleasure in the children, but she found them tiresome after protracted periods of time. She clearly remembered when both children, a son and a daughter, had been four and two years old and she had had the impression that there was no time in her life for anything other than the kids. That was the first time "she felt really claustrophobic," and she told her husband that something had to change. The two of them then worked out an arrangement whereby she could work on three afternoons, instead of just one, in her boutique. She had astonishingly little to say about her now grownup children. She didn't even know, for example, the address of the share-house where her son had already been living for more than four months.

At first it seemed that here was a mother who had a good deal of respect for her children's independent lives ("I was always careful to make sure that they became independent quickly, and butted in as little as possible"), but more and more, the picture turned into that of a mother who was no longer the least bit interested in her children. Then again, this image conflicted with the image I had of her as a mother when her children were growing up. It is true, she was concerned with fostering her children's independence, as she herself stressed, but at the same time she was thoroughly concerned with their well-being. One could see evidence of this in the way that she staged her own version of films that the children particularly liked, together with their friends, replete with home-made costumes.

I began to suspect that Angela had somehow got stuck in the phase of not wanting to admit what was happening, that she was denying her interest in her children rather than accepting the fact of the separation. It was almost as though her children had died. I articulated this sentiment in therapy, "It almost seems to me that your children have died." This sentence gave her an enormous fright, all the more so because her son had recently said to her that a person could die and she wouldn't know anything about it.

She could now see that she had simply repressed the whole separation process, largely thanks to the fact that she had plunged herself into the work at her boutique. Her husband had reacted similarly. He, too, had just made himself independent along with a colleague, and they were overworked with plans and worries about the future.

It also became clear to Angela that it was part of her nature to rather unsentimentally declare something at an end. By reacting this way, there was less opportunity for all kinds of emotional complications to surface. For this reason, the dependable camaraderie of her husband was so dear to her.

Once Angela became aware of the extent of her repression, initially she felt enormous pity for her children whom she had treated so sorely. Inwardly, she apologized to them. Outwardly, she carefully began to try to get close to them again. I felt that it was important for her to first solve the problem within herself, rather than to just throw herself at the children. The children were after all just in the process of separating and setting up boundaries themselves. They only complained about the fact that their mother demonstrated so little interest in them, and also maintained that the boutique was their mother's "favorite child." The topic of guilt also came up for Angela. She asked herself whether she had been a good enough mother. Ought she perhaps not to have had any children if she wasn't going to be "such a passionate mother?" She asked herself the question that all working mothers ask themselves, whether she had kept a reasonable balance between motherhood and professional life, whether such a "double burden" was justifiable at all, and so on. Ultimately, she found her own solution to the problem. She knew very well that life as a housewife was not satisfying, that it would not have been fulfilling, and that she would probably have been a considerably more impatient mother had she not had her own work that satisfied her. She could also reassure herself with the knowledge that her husband participated in the life of the children, that—if need be—he could also have given her more support. However, since both children gave the impression of being content, in time she found that she could relinquish these guilt feelings and try to find an appropriate outlook for the next phase of life.

She, too, had an enormous unconscious rage against her children. She was angry with them because they had been able to build their own lives, had started off with far better prospects than she, their mother, had ever had. They were so much more relaxed in their approach to life, they tried out many more things, and lived in a much more creative way. Her envy of her children became tangible, and her unproductive way of dealing with her feelings was clear from her attitude towards them. Again and again, she expressed the opinion that they should have to work really hard for a change, so that they would see what it was like to have "the money stuffed up their backsides(!)" and so on. In other words, rather than dealing with the problem, she just wanted to get rid of the source of the envy.

What was the root of all this aggression? In the context of memory work, I asked her to think about ways in which the children had enriched her life. She told me enthusiastically about how the children had fostered her own creativity—at all different levels. The older children, in particular, when they were eighteen or twenty, had had all kinds of creative ideas. They had brought their creative friends home, sometimes real screwballs, and had talked about their projects. This had always generated an inspired atmosphere at home and there had been a tangible, if not actually articulated conviction that almost anything was possible in the world. She talked herself into a reverie and then said suddenly, "And this doesn't exist anymore, not since our children have moved away from home, it's all just gone. I hold it against them, I envy them." When she became aware that she was in pain over the loss of this quality of life, the envy in her dissipated. She sensed what it was that she now missed in life and realized that it wasn't just something that one could get any old place. In good moments, she was thankful for the fact that she had at least had the opportunity to experience it. She was also aware that a creative side had been awakened in her. But at the same time, being more or less compelled on a daily basis to interact with creative young people and their castles in the air, something that can, of course, also be completely enervating at times, is nevertheless not the same as being aware that one is capable of generating a creative, inspired atmosphere on one's own.

Angela now realized why she suddenly found her husband so boring. She expected him to replace the inspiring atmosphere for her. This, however, was not something he was capable of doing, especially since he was pressured with his own worries. It was also impossible for him to single-handedly generate the atmosphere that all these young people had produced in consort. In fact, it turned out that he too missed the atmosphere. He may have been significantly less enthused by it than his wife, but he did find it stimulating; even though he thought she was often "very unrealistic," "a dreamer," or "a nutcase."

This process of belated grieving was accomplished in a relatively short period of time. Angela attended about twenty therapy sessions with me. Once the grieving process had been initiated she could do the rest herself, through conversations with her husband, with her children, and with other women who were in the same position themselves. Angela had a non-derivative identity that she could use to reconstitute herself, an identity that also allowed her to change. She realized that something in her life was now fundamentally different. She also suffered more than she had before by virtue of the fact that she could no longer see herself as the rational person she had once been. She noticed that she was always plagued by contradictory feelings. She had, for example, the desire to see her children become autonomous and strong, particularly her daughter; on the other hand, she also wished that her children would stay a little dependent so that she would not lose all her sense of importance. She spent a lot of time thinking about how she might be able to recreate those hours of inspiration, albeit in more moderate proportions.

IN HEIDI'S CASE, the separation process was quite different. Heidi has five sons. A teacher, Heidi was also initially employed part-time. Then when her youngest son was fifteen, she was employed at eighty percent of a full-time workload. Heidi is fifty-three when she enters therapy. She feels that her life is empty, meaningless; she feels overwhelmed by the tremendous demands placed on her by her family and her job. She feels overextended and regards this as being the reason why she "is fed-up with life." She does not know how she can resist the onslaught. She has the feeling that even though she is exhausted, she really does have to "fight on all fronts." Her choice of words shows that she feels that she is embroiled in a war, yet the main conflicts are not addressed. She only says that she feels that too many demands are placed on her, that she feels alone in her family surrounded by all those men. For this reason, she likes to work as a teacher in a girls' school. She is waiting for the day when someone comes to her and tells her what she should do, or better still, asks what they can do for her. Her husband shows little understanding for her situation. He finds her reaction paradoxical: while all the boys were at home, she managed to get far more done and without as much stress. Now that only the youngest is still there, everything is too much for her.

In conversation, it seemed that she transferred her husband's opinions onto me, then her sons' opinions, and also those of her colleagues at the school. Aside from the fact that she said that she felt exhausted, she made hardly any statements that actually concerned her personally. She spoke in a distanced and measured way about her problem.

I think about her husband's statement to the effect that she obviously felt better when her sons were still at home. And so I ask her to tell me something about this period of time. She speaks enthusiastically about her children and she talks about the conflict she felt between her professional life and her duties as a mother. But since her husband, also a teacher, had loved to help with family life, the responsibilities could be shared between the two of them. Her husband had always been successful in reassuring her that she really could accomplish both things. He had also been the one to encourage her to take up her profession again. She had had a close, tender relationship with her sons. This had changed, however, when they were seventeen or eighteen and had started to associate more with their peers. All of a sudden they became "louts." There is an angry edge to her voice, but also some sadness. She had had a particularly close relationship with two of her sons. They had always given her the feeling that she was a really first class woman. They had told her, for example, what clothes she should wear, what particularly suited her. Now it was these very sons who had developed a close and exclusive relationship, and she hardly saw the two of them any more. As she said this she sunk down even more into herself. It was clear from what she had said that her sons somehow guaranteed her self-worth as a woman and that this reassurance was now lacking. She could not, however, express it as such, and in general she was extraordinarily angry about the "exclusive" relationship that these sons cultivated. She was jealous but was not able to admit that this was how she felt. Intellectually she could actually appreciate that her "depressive exhaustion" had something to do with the separation of the children. This weighed on her, all the more so when her husband also had trouble dealing with the situation. Emotionally, however, she could not even begin to access all the feelings of grief and of anger. In her case, as with my other clients, it was a matter of using dreams, fantasies, transference, and counter-transference to help her find her own, non-derivative identity. Only later, was she able to admit what a loss it was to her when these tender boys suddenly turned into men and became the spitting image of the others; what a loss it was when she realized that she was no longer the most important thing in the world to her two favorite sons.

The fact that she worked was helpful to her during this difficult time of life. Work structured her life. She was simply forced by circumstance to attend to certain duties. For a while, that gave her a frame of reference. Had she been left up to her own devices, she would not have had any idea where to begin, no interests and no desires, especially since her husband was reluctant to continue dictating what she should do. Only after a long period of therapy did she begin to know what she herself wanted, what interested her.

Heidi was the daughter of an energetic, dynamic teacher who dominated his wife and who made sure that everything followed its prescribed course. Heidi's mother was a retiring person and stayed in the background. She advised her daughter that it was good to marry early, and this is just what Heidi did. Her husband, who had at first worked at something else, trained as a teacher during the first few years of married life. It was also true in Heidi's case, that there had neither been conflict with her mother and father and the ensuing separation, nor had Heidi taken issue with their various viewpoints on life. Her depressive constitution had been encouraged, and she strongly identified with her mother, which fostered a lifestyle that, at least initially, was thoroughly satisfying to her.

Working mothers, like mothers who stay at home, have their own difficulties in separating from the children. However, they do have the advantage of not being exclusively fixated on the mothering role.

# The Difficult Separation from Difficult Children

◆

IN THE EXAMPLES THAT I CHOSE, the children had all more or less "turned out alright"—at least according to their mothers' reports. By doing memory work with these mothers, we repeatedly established that each of these children really had evoked fundamental personality traits in the mothers, or at least had brought liveliness into the home—in itself, no small order. Common to all of these separation processes was the fact that people experienced feelings of guilt. Guilt feelings reflect the fact that as human beings we are always indebted to one another for something and that we just have to stay indebted. And so, of course, it is not just children who owe their parents; mothers also owe their children something. In the case of all the aforementioned women, the separation process in a therapeutic context came to an end once these mothers recognized the richness of their lives. They no longer felt deprived of life. Instead, they were resolved to bring their mothering role to an end—or at least provisionally to an end—a task that had been meaningful, worthwhile, and which had absorbed them for a certain period of their lives. Despite feeling gratitude for everything they had experienced with the children, and in spite of being thankful that the relationship could continue in an amended form, these mothers were now aware that they had certain reservations about their grown children. One mother, for example, thought that her son was really egotistical in his relationship with her. Another mother had difficulty dealing with her daughter's straight-forward pronouncement to the effect that having children would annoy her horribly. However, the mother's reservations were no longer expressed as demands for change in the relationship, but rather were accepted as being characteristic of different lifestyles. Their children's individual qualities were accepted in the same way that they might be accepted in other people who were not part of the family. The mothers made it quite clear that some quality or other was undesirable, but nevertheless, they let their daughters and sons know that they were still worthy of being loved.

One can think of it like this: if the reservations we have about our children are not followed up with "suggestions for improvement," then we really do show them that we respect the autonomy of the younger generation. If we can live by this credo, then we have comprehended that people are loveable even when they possess qualities we do not like.

However, separation is made considerably more difficult when one has the impression that one has had a lifetime of difficulties with a child, that the child has not brought anything lovable into our lives, that the child has not evoked anything in us that we could look back on with joy and thankfulness. Instead, we are consumed by feelings of powerlessness, rage, and guilt.

How does separation look when one does not see oneself as having been basically a good parent, when it seems pretty clear that one has in actual fact failed? What is it like to try to separate when one feels guilty because of this failure, and one turns the adolescents into scapegoats in order to avoid having to deal with one's own shortcomings? It is this very defense mechanism that intensifies the problem: the "scapegoats" are often forced into "guilty" behavior. These children are more or less delegated the role of acting out.[27]

It is extraordinarily difficult for us to accept the problematic sides of ourselves, particularly when these problematic sides have far-reaching consequences in the lives of other people. We try to find others who we think are just as much to blame for the consequences of our failures as we are, or perhaps we look for people who we think are wholly to blame for the entire mess. Or then again, we repress our feelings of guilt. We may, for example, suffer from an exaggerated fear that we will be injured or die a premature death. The anger that we feel towards ourselves (but will not admit to) can instead be manifest through these fantasies. Our own disguised death wish is then experienced as an exaggerated fear of death. The attempt to repress our fundamental dissatisfaction with ourselves is fostered by the culture in which we live. Rather than dealing with issues head-on, success is sought in some other aspect of life. Indeed, high-profile success, generally material success, is seen as being the most desirable.

In pursuing success, one may feel somewhat better in the short-term, but the separation problem is not solved as a result. One remains stuck with one's feelings of anger, guilt, and fear.

Separation and the grieving process associated with it can only take place once we are able to acknowledge our guilt. We also have to learn to understand why we had to become so guilty in the first place. This capacity to be honest with oneself even when things go wrong (or at least wrong in terms of the ideals and expectations that we place on ourselves) presupposes that we are able to accept our own shadow-sides. In accepting our shadow-sides, we relate to an identity that knows light and shade, that is comprised of both light and dark. This means that we accept ourselves even when we fall short of what we are capable of. Only when we are able to do this, can we hope to see the life possibilities that are still available to us.

Such precise self-scrutiny requires an enormous amount of courage. Self-analysis is especially difficult when we consciously, or unconsciously, know that we have made a mistake, when we know that we will continue to make mistakes, and perhaps be forced to make mistakes because there is no right answer. When we know that we are in the wrong, we often have a need to appease our strained feelings of self-worth. We might, for example, try to raise our feelings of self-worth by idealizing our own talents or by idealizing a path that we have taken. In contrast, self-analysis does not make us feel better. At least initially, it can hurt. In the long-run, however, it is a way of being able to deal with the problem so that we find ourselves engaged in a process, and not languishing in a *cul-de-sac*. Such reflection is also important with regards to the development of one's own identity: we always live as who we are, and not as who we pretend to be. By knowingly living as who we are, we feel identical with ourselves, true and vital, and, as such, are well on the way to acquiring an increasingly authentic, autonomous identity.

ERIKA, FIFTY-SIX, has great difficulty separating from her children, particularly from her eldest daughter. This daughter can do no right, as far as Erika is concerned. After two abortions, which Erika profoundly condemned, the daughter decided when she became pregnant again that she would have the child, albeit out of wedlock. She maintained that she did not know who the father of the child was. Erika was critical of this as well. She told her daughter in no uncertain terms, that she ought not count on her doing the slightest thing to help the little brat. Her daughter complained about this, and reiterated something she had obviously said a lot during her childhood and adolescence (the daughter is now thirty-three), "You just don't love me. You have something against me. No matter what I do, you are never satisfied."

During therapy, Erika indignantly complained about her daughter and made it clear that she simply could not accept her daughter's lifestyle: all her many affairs since early adolescence; the link between promiscuity and her excessive consumption of alcohol; the way she "incessantly" changed jobs (the daughter had been employed for two years at her last job).

Erika can in no way, shape, or form say that she agrees with her daughter's lifestyle; absolutely nothing is acceptable about her life. The daughter, on the other hand, always seems to be waiting for her mother to come around and agree with her.

I try to do memory work with Erika by encouraging her to explore the qualities that her daughter may have animated in her. This prompts an enormous outburst: her daughter has taken all the pleasure out of her life. Erika did not abort the baby, and because of her, agreed to marry a problematic man, from whom she is now divorced. The only thanks she gets from her daughter are all the problems that she causes. Even as a baby, she always screamed, would not be put to sleep at night; later she was head-strong, had difficulties in school, told lies, stole, all attempts to rear her properly were in vain. In telling this story, Erika says that she has sacrificed an incredible amount for this child, and that it was all completely useless. Rather than feeling grateful, she feels punished by the child—punished through and through. From her story one can see that she cannot admit to herself that she has never really loved her daughter. She does not acknowledge that she, too, has a role to play in the troubles with her daughter, and that the pregnancy with her all those years ago must have placed her in a very difficult position. Aside from this, Erika stabilizes her sense of self-worth by comparing her course of action back then with her daughter's actions today. As a result, Erika comes across as being "virtuous," whereas she disqualifies her daughter's actions today as being unethical.

Over the course of several weeks, Erika speaks in therapy about the time just after she had conceived her first daughter, about her problems, her doubts, and her feeling of being all alone. At the time, Erika's partner thought it best just to marry quickly and the problem would be solved. She realized very quickly that she could not really disagree with her husband, especially not as far as the relationship was concerned. As far as he was concerned, there simply were no problems. In time, the tone of Erika's story changed. She was no longer so concerned with idealizing her decision to have the child, nor so intent on talking about the ensuing consequences she had had to put up with until the youngest child was fully grown. Slowly but surely she developed an empathy for the woman she had been and for the situation she had found herself in. At the time, she had barely been able to conquer the situation and had felt terribly alone. With this growing empathy for herself, Erika was also better able to empathize with her daughter. Finally, during an altercation between mother and daughter in which the daughter once again complained about the absence of motherly love, Erika was able to admit that it was true, she had never loved her. And she told her daughter what it had meant to her not to have had an abortion and to have only married because of her. Erika expected to be hated for this revelation, yet her daughter responded as though she had been released, "almost lovingly" is how Erika described it. Erika's daughter now had confirmation of something that she had long and frequently sensed, something that she had also reconciled herself to, but which until now had never been confirmed by her mother. Apparently, Erika was also able to express to her daughter the awareness that they had both had a very rough time with one another, and that they would probably continue to have a difficult time.

There followed a phase in which Erika thought that all her daughter's difficulties were caused by her. She suffered terribly from guilt feelings. Fortunately, we had already processed her story in good, understandable terms, so that this positive perspective could always be drawn upon. Erika now learned to look at the ways in which she was still to blame, the times when she would totally reject her daughter. After a phase during which she tried to understand everything her daughter did, even to idealize her for things that she had spent so many years denouncing, this was more prevalent.

Erika was very sorry that she had treated her daughter unlovingly for so long, and now tried to behave in a more loving manner. She also felt guilty when she behaved unlovingly. Nevertheless, it was still difficult for her to accept that having given up so much in order to live her life "right," she could have a daughter who led a "ruined existence." She had difficulty supporting her in front of other people. In a conversation with one of her other children, she became aware that she also had her marriage to thank for these other children. And these children had given her lots of pleasure. As a result, she saw her decision not to have an abortion in a somewhat different light. She realized that at the time, she had only had two impossible choices, the opportunity to make two mistakes, as she put it. She ended up choosing the one which seemed the most appropriate to her, and that was now the fate that she and her daughter had to live with.

The entire problematic association with her daughter—to the extent she was still burdened by it—came to represent her whole course of life and the fact that she had to take responsibility for her own life. By taking control she felt a much stronger sense of self-worth. Mother and daughter had entered into a mutual dialogue, albeit a painful one.

After Erika could admit to herself that she had not

loved her daughter, that she would rather have wiped her out of her life, the memory work about the time they had shared could proceed very differently than before. Suddenly it occurred to Erika that her daughter had had a very caring side to her personality, that she had sometimes brought her mother berries or a piece of fruit just when she was feeling really exhausted. And that had happened often. She also remembered that her daughter never cared what other people thought and had thereby introduced an element of freedom into the family. This may well be the reason that the other children in the family find this "wayward sister" less terrible than their mother does, and are also prepared to help her out when need be.

This memory work in the context of a very difficult relationship shows something that is actually true for all such situations, namely that there is no child that only creates problems, that only evokes unpleasantness. There are, however, many relationships where so many feelings are repressed and denied and so much unconscious hatred ferments, that loving feelings can no longer be accessed. As a result, memories of things that have animated and stimulated us are also repressed.

Erika found that her life was more lively, that as a person she was more real, once she could accept that she had made some very grave mistakes. She could now acknowledge her errors and could see and accept their consequences.

# The Central Question of
# Identity

◆

EVERY INSTANCE OF GRIEF, every separation process, every parting, every loss compels human beings to think about themselves in a new light. We are forced to consider our own identity and to redefine it so that it reflects the change in life circumstances. Without this process of readjustment, one comes to the frightening realization that one's own identity is no longer tenable. When we examine the identity problems that arise, when we ask ourselves questions about who we are in the current context, when we ask what is left, what is valid, what we are, and what we would like to have been, it becomes clear that separations are forced on us by life and they require us to be introspective. In being introspective, we become increasingly true to ourselves, increasingly autonomous and authentic, and as such, increasingly capable of having healthy relationships.

The problems that some women have in separating from their children show that certain things are long overdue. They show that it is high time the woman takes a good hard look at her own identity, that she has to catch up, that long due changes to her identity have to be set in motion. Women, who for the most part have lived with a derivative, "prescribed" identity, must first find their own autonomous identity.

Obviously the search for an independent identity can be delayed in the life of a woman. It cannot, however, be avoided. And the later a woman posits the question of her own identity, the more difficult it will be for her to find out what might hold true for the rest of her life, and figure out what there still is to experience. The grief over the unlived life grows and grows. To be sure, every course of life precludes certain other possibilities—all human beings have to grieve for the life they could not live.

And so, the separation process from the children, like any other separation process, is really a calling, an opportunity to know oneself better, and to think of oneself in a new light.

# Notes

..

[1]*Züri-Woche*, June 28, 1990.

[2]Evelyn Mastow and P. Newberry, "Work role and depression in women: A comparison of workers and housewives in treatment," in *American Journal of Arthopsychiatry* 45 (1975):538–548.

[3]Adolescence: Early adolescence falls between the ages of roughly fourteen and eighteen. It is characterized by the choice of a profession, and so on. In later adolescence (between the ages of eighteen and twenty-one), the role of an adult is slowly assumed. Of central importance are the issues of independence and separating from the family of origin.

[4]Cf. Rubin and Gertrude Blanck, *Angewandte Ich-Psychologie* (Stuttgart, 1978), 56 ff.

[5]Cf. Margaret S. Mahler, *Symbiose und Individuation* (Stuttgart, 1972).

[6]Verena Kast, *Wege zur Autonomie: Märchen psychologisch gedeutet* (Olten, Freiburg im Breisgau, 1986).

[7]Kast, *Trauern: Phasen und Chancen des psychischen Prozesses* (Stuttgart, 1990).

[8]Kast, *Paare: Beziehungsphantasien oder Wie Götter sich in Menschen spiegeln* (Stuttgart, 1990).

[9]Clive S. Lewis, *Über die Trauer* (Zürich, 1990).

[10]Kast, *Die Dynamik der Symbole: Grundlage der Jungschen Psychotherapie* (Olten, Freiburg im Breisgau, 1990), 198–203.

[11]Archetype: The archetype is both a structural and a dynamic factor in the psychic and physical realms. This means that psychic and physical processes operate within a certain human type; in certain situations, human beings have comparable images, emotions, and drives. The unconscious archetype conjures up not only similar images, but also similar instinctive and physical reactions. It is an inexorable part of being human that the individual has a mother and a father, and that he or she always looks for them if they are not on hand. All human beings are also capable of developing motherly and fatherly characteristics. These archetypal representations are, however, always transmitted by way of our personal complexes, through our own personal experiences of father and mother. This explains why an archetypical situation will be conditioned by a strong personal element. Cf. Kast, *Dynamik der Symbole*, 115.

[12]Helm Stierman et al., "Problemfamilien" in "Erstinterview" in Helm Stierlin und Josef Duss-von Werdt (eds.), *Familiendynamik* 3, (Stuttgart, 1977), 221 f.

[13]Cf. Kast, *Dynamik der Symbole*, see Komplex.

[14]Kast, *Trauern*.

[15]Parts of the following text have been drawn from my book, *Die Dynamik der Symbole*, 68 ff., and appear in an abbreviated, slightly modified form.

[16]Shadows: The term designates sides of ourselves that we cannot accept, that do not correspond to our own ego-ideal. We repress these aspects of ourselves and are then predisposed to see them in other people. In projecting these aspects of ourselves onto other people, we are also inclined to struggle with them there. Apart from personal shadows, there are also collective shadows.

On personal shadows: People who like to think of themselves as being generous, harbor their pettiness as a shadow; people who think they are not aggressive, have aggression in their shadows. When this shadow is manifest, then such people may act in an aggressive manner, but just not realize that they are doing so. The shadow shows us that we are not the way we would like to think we are. It confronts us with the fact that we are also the very thing that we consciously decide against, that our opposite is also harbored in the soul. Cf. Kast, *Dynamik der Symbole*, 242–244.

[17]Cf. Kast, *Dynamik der Symbole*, 13 ff.

[18]Claudia Bernardoni and Vera Werder, "Erfolg statt Karriere," in *Ohne Seil und Haken: Frauen auf dem Weg nach oben* (Munich, 1990).

[19]Cf. Kast, *Paare*, see Anima.

[20]Sandra Scarr, *Wenn Mütter arbeiten: Wie Kinder und Beruf sich verbinden lassen* (Munich, 1987).

[21]Martin Seligman, *Erlernte Hilflosigkeit* (Stuttgart, 1979).

[22]Christa Rohde-Dachser, "Weiblichkeitsparadigmen in der Psychoanalyse," in Karola Brede (ed.), *Was will das Weib in mir* (Freiburg im Breisgau, 1989), 94 ff.

[23]Ingrid Riedel, *Die weise Frau in uralt neuen Erfahrungen* (Olten, 1989).

[24]Kast, *Paare*, see Bruder Mann und Schwester Frau.

[25]Kast, *Dynamik der Symbole*.

[26]Kast, *Imagination als Raum der Freiheit: Dialog zwischen Ich und Unbewußtem* (Walter, Olten, 1988).

[27]Zum Thema der Schuldproblematik. Cf. Kast, *Dynamik der Symbole*.